Acing the LLB

Acing the LLB

Acing the LLB

Capturing Your Full Potential to Improve Your Grades

JOHN McGARRY

 Routledge
Taylor & Francis Group

LONDON AND NEW YORK

First published 2016
by Routledge
2 Park Square, Milton Park, Abingdon, Oxon, OX14 4RN

and by Routledge
711 Third Avenue, New York, NY 10017

Routledge is an imprint of the Taylor & Francis Group, an informa business

British Library Cataloguing in Publication Data
A catalogue record for this book is available from the British Library

Library of Congress Cataloging-in-Publication Data
McGarry, John (Law teacher), author.
  Acing the LLB / John McGarry.
  pages cm
  Includes bibliographical references.
  ISBN 978-1-138-85347-8 (hbk) -- ISBN 978-1-138-85352-2 (pbk) -- ISBN
  978-1-315-71331-1 (ebk) 1. Law--Study and teaching--United States. 2.
  Law students--United States. 3. Law--Vocational guidance--United
  States. I. Title.
  KF272.M277 2016
  340.071'173--dc23
  2015034096

ISBN: 978–1–138–85347–8 (hbk)
ISBN: 978–1–138–85352–2 (pbk)
ISBN: 978–1–315–71331–1 (ebk)

Typeset in Vectora LH by
Florence Production Ltd, Stoodleigh, Devon, UK

Printed and bound in Great Britain by
TJ International Ltd, Padstow, Cornwall

For Alex

Contents

Acknowledgements

I would first like to thank the staff at Routledge for commissioning the book, advising me about the title and content, guiding me through the different stages of the process and tolerating my deadline stretching, especially Fiona Briden, Damian Mitchell and Emily Wells.

I would also like to thank those colleagues in my own and other institutions who allowed me to interview them and make use of their comments and thoughts: Andrea Cerevkova, Clare Kinsella, Peter Langford, Sharon McAvoy, Adam Pendlebury, Samantha Spence and Kas Wachala. In addition, I thank other colleagues with whom I have worked over the years, and the students whom I have taught, for all that I have learned from them.

I thank my friends – particularly Phillipa Malone, Gavin Muir, Alex Muir and Alison Haughton – for, among other things, distracting me with alcohol and gossip. I also thank my family, Joan, Ken, Clare and Joe. As ever, my wife and son deserve, and have, the greatest share of my gratitude: Clare, who has borne the brunt of the household and child rearing duties while I have been completing this text, and Joe, who has not had as much of my time as he deserved. I would not have completed this without their patience and love.

Introduction

For most students, undertaking a law degree is a challenging, and even daunting, prospect. Most will be new to higher-education study and many will be new to the study of law. Even those who have studied some law before will find themselves: studying new subjects; expected to acquire and deploy new skills; assessed in new ways; and generally operating at a higher level, and with greater intensity, than they will have been used to. Further, often, students do not realise what is required of them to get better marks and what they should do to avoid making common errors.

This book aims to help readers navigate their way through their time as a law student. It is not meant as a replacement for your substantive law textbooks (e.g. your contract law or tort law textbooks); rather, my intention is that it is supplementary to these books. My purpose is to provide general information and practical advice that will help enhance your chances of attaining the best marks and avoiding mistakes.

My writing of the book has been motivated by my experience as a lecturer. Year after year, I encounter students who, despite being very capable, do not reach their potential until very late in their degree, or perhaps not even at all. Often this is because, although they are putting lots of effort into their work, they are not working smart enough and are lacking in some practical ways. Frustration at witnessing students make errors or fail to take some elementary steps by which they could improve their work and receive better marks has been the driving force in my desire to collate and offer the range of tips, techniques and guidance that I offer to my own students.

In writing this text, I have drawn on my own time as a lecturer as well as the experience of those with whom I have taught over the years. In particular, I have interviewed colleagues who have allowed me to share their thoughts and ideas about how students may improve their marks, what they should avoid doing and, even, what – as lecturers – their pet hates are.

Throughout the book, I use diagrams and other features to help me convey my message and make it more accessible. These include:

LECTURERS' THOUGHTS

These are excerpts from my interviews with colleagues that are used throughout the book to emphasise and reinforce the points being made. I have used pseudonyms in place of my colleagues' real names to maintain their anonymity.

	LECTURERS' THOUGHTS
Anna	When marking coursework, I ask myself four basic questions': 1 Has the student answered the question? 2 Does the student know what they are talking about? 3 Have they put the effort in? 4 Is it well written, well presented and correctly referenced?'

TIP BOXES

These are designed to give students relevant practical advice.

TIP BOX

When writing coursework, use the find function on your word processing programme to look for words which you often misspell. For instance, if you commonly write 'statue' instead of 'statute' use the find function to see if the word 'statue' is in your work.

COMMON ERROR

The common error feature is used to inform readers of mistakes that students often make and, if necessary, give advice about how to avoid them. So, the following example is taken from Chapter 7, which gives advice about exams:

COMMON ERROR

Do not spend more time on one question at the expense of the others. The extra marks you earn by spending more time on one will probably not compensate for those you lose by spending less time on another.

LECTURERS' PET HATES

This feature draws on my interviews with colleagues who were asked what their pet hates about certain things are. It also draws on my own experience and knowledge of what colleagues and I dislike.

LECTURERS' PET HATES

'In seminars, it's so annoying when students aren't able to tell you even the most basic details about a case [that they have been asked to read beforehand] without reading from their notes or, even worse, from a textbook. They should have this stuff at their fingertips, ready to go'.

WORK SMARTER

The work smarter feature, as the name suggests, supplies the reader with advice about how they can make the most of their time and studies.

WORK SMARTER

Try to read your lecture notes within an hour or so of the end of the lecture and the relevant pages of your textbook within a day or two after the class. This will reinforce your memory of the lecture, aid your understanding and make it easier to recall the information when you need it.

The book is made up of eleven chapters, each one designed to take you through the key aspects of being a law student:

CHAPTER 1: UNDERSTANDING AND MAKING THE MOST OF YOUR DEGREE

The purpose of this chapter is to enable students to understand the nature and structure of degrees in general and law degrees in particular. It:

- explains the different subjects that compose a law degree, including the difference between foundational, core and optional subjects;
- gives advice about choosing which optional subjects to study;
- explains the roles of the different staff whom they are likely to encounter, such as programme leaders and module leaders;
- explains degree classifications; and
- explains the role of the marker, second marker and external examiner.

This chapter also advises readers how best to work with their lecturers to get the most from them and discusses the benefits of engaging in extracurricular activities, such as joining their institution's student law society, attending lectures by visiting speakers and entering mooting competitions.

CHAPTER 2: GETTING THE MOST OUT OF YOUR CLASSES

In Chapter 2, readers are introduced to the two main types of class that they will encounter as law students: lectures and seminars. The chapter explains what is expected of students in these classes. It also suggests how they can best prepare for them, how they can get the most from them and what they can do afterwards to improve their recall and understanding.

CHAPTER 3: READING AND INDEPENDENT STUDY

Chapter 3 discusses the importance of reading and independent study. It introduces students to the difference between primary materials (cases and legislation) and secondary materials (textbooks, journal articles and the like) and provides a brief description of the different types of secondary material that students will encounter. It also gives advice about reading and understanding both primary and secondary materials. The chapter concludes with a table giving the meaning and usage of some of the most common Latin terms employed in legal and academic writing.

CHAPTER 4: AN INTRODUCTION TO ASSESSMENTS

This chapter introduces students to the main types and methods of assessment that they are likely to encounter when studying law. It also considers academic malpractice – such as plagiarism – and gives advice about how to avoid it. Finally, it discusses the importance of obtaining, and acting on, feedback on the work they produce.

CHAPTER 5: UNDERSTANDING ESSAY QUESTIONS AND PROBLEM QUESTIONS

Here, readers are introduced to the two main types of question that they will meet on a law degree: essay questions and problem questions. Through the use of examples, they will be given advice about the structure of these questions, about how to understand them and about understanding what they are being asked.

CHAPTER 6: ANSWERING COURSEWORK QUESTIONS

This chapter discusses what lecturers are looking for when marking coursework and how students can plan and structure their answers and ensure that they address the question asked. It discusses the importance of reading a variety of materials to inform your work. It also gives advice about writing style and structure and about how best to proofread work so that it is free of mistakes.

CHAPTER 7: EXAMS

In Chapter 7, the reader is introduced to the different types of exam that they may come across as a law student. The chapter looks at the expectations of those who mark exams. It also advises students on how they may prepare for, and make the best use of their time during, exams. In addition, it considers some techniques that students may employ to deal with nerves.

CHAPTER 8: PRESENTATIONS, MOOTS AND ASSESSED SEMINARS

In this chapter, we discuss what markers are looking for when marking presentations, moots and assessed seminars. The chapter offers advice about how students may prepare for these types of assessment. It discusses: how students may structure their presentation, the use of presentation software and other visual aids, how to deal with questions that may be asked when they are presenting or mooting, how to dress and how to practise. It also explains the etiquette of mooting. The final section considers assessed seminars and how students may perform at their best in them.

CHAPTER 9: DISSERTATIONS

This chapter advises readers about different aspects of undertaking dissertation research, including: a brief explanation of research; advice about choosing a dissertation topic; writing a dissertation proposal; an explanation of methods and methodology; an explanation of the nature of, and advice about undertaking, a literature review; advice about how to get the best out of the supervision process; and how to manage their time.

CHAPTER 10: REFERENCING AND BIBLIOGRAPHY

Chapter 10 discusses the importance of referencing and advises readers about how to reference and what is required for a bibliography. It also provides information about the use of quotations.

CHAPTER 11: AFTER YOUR DEGREE

This chapter discusses the routes that a law graduate might take to become a practising lawyer, say, a barrister, solicitor, legal executive or paralegal. It also considers other careers law graduates might enter. The chapter gives advice on drafting a CV and covering letter. Finally, the chapter looks at various postgraduate qualifications and explains how they differ from one another.

I really do hope that working with the text helps you, the reader, to get the best out of yourself, your institution and your law degree studies. All that is left at this stage is to wish you good luck!

Chapter 1
Understanding and making the most of your degree

This chapter:

- explains what a qualifying law degree is;
- describes the difference between foundational, optional and core subjects;
- advises students about choosing optional subjects;
- explains the role of different staff involved in the delivery of a law degree, such as: programme leaders, module leaders and external examiners;
- describes the different degree classifications and the marks that are usually required for each;
- advises readers about how they may best work with lecturers to get the most from them;
- discusses the value of joining student societies and engaging in other extracurricular activities.

1.1   INTRODUCTION

For most students, beginning their law degree will be their first direct experience of higher education. Much of what they encounter will be new or, at the very least, different to the ways in which they have previously been taught. Moreover, even for those who have studied at higher-education level before, or who have previously studied some law, undertaking a law degree will be a significant and new experience.

This chapter introduces you to degrees in general, and law degrees in particular. It discusses the roles of the different staff who are involved in your degree and how you can best work with them. It also explains the way degrees are classified. The chapter concludes by considering the benefits of becoming involved in different extracurricular activities, such as joining the student law society, attending lectures by visiting speakers and entering mooting competitions.

Throughout this chapter, and in other places in the book, I will emphasise the importance of treating the staff of your institution – whether academic, administrative, catering, housekeeping, maintenance or security staff – and your fellow students with courtesy and respect. This is, of course, the right and decent way to behave in itself. It is also the smart way to behave – you will be doing your degree over a number of years and, at times, you might need the help and advice of those around you. Such help is more likely to be forthcoming if you have behaved considerately towards others.

1.2   A QUALIFYING LAW DEGREE

I have written this book with the assumption that its primary readership will comprise those studying, or planning to study, for a qualifying law degree. The book will, though, be useful for anyone studying law.

A qualifying law degree is one that has been approved by the Solicitors Regulation Authority and the Bar Council as satisfying the academic stage of training for those wanting to become solicitors or barristers. That is, it is sanctioned as the first step you can take to become a practising solicitor or barrister. (Chapter 11 gives details about what else is required to qualify as a barrister or solicitor and about what other legal and non-legal careers law graduates may pursue.)

Those who complete the qualifying law degree are usually entitled to place the letters LLB after their name. As a point of interest, LLB is an abbreviation of *Legum Baccalaureus*, which means Bachelor of Laws – just as those taking a science degree would become a Bachelor of Science (BSc), and those taking an arts degree would become a Bachelor of Arts (BA).

1.2.1   Foundational, core and optional subjects

In order to be classified as a qualifying law degree, students must study the seven foundational law subjects. They may also be required to study some core subjects and will have some optional subjects available to them.

Foundational subjects

There are seven foundational subjects that you must study for the qualifying law degree:

- contract law
- tort law
- criminal law
- equity and trusts
- European Union law
- property law
- constitutional and administrative law.

In some institutions, these foundational subjects may be given other names. For instance, property law is sometimes referred to as land law, and constitutional and administrative law may be known as public law. Further, the precise content of these subjects may vary from institution to institution – usually because they will reflect the research and interests of the lecturers teaching them. So, in one institution, you may study the role of the UK monarchy as part of constitutional and administrative law, whereas it may not be examined at all in another.

Moreover, rather than be studied as separate, discrete subjects, two or more of the foundational subjects may be combined into one module. So, rather than

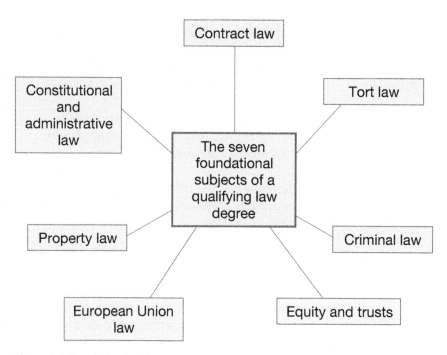

Figure 1.1 Foundational subjects

contract and tort law being studied separately, they may be combined in one module, entitled, for instance, the law of obligations.

Core subjects

In addition to the foundational subjects, there may be some subjects that your institution requires you to study and pass in order to obtain the degree. These are known as core subjects. So, for example, most law degrees will require you to study a module that examines the legal system or one that provides you with certain lawyers' skills (such as legal research and the like). It is also increasingly common for students of all subjects to have to take modules designed to improve their employability and personal development.

Optional subjects

After the foundational and core subjects, the remainder of your degree will be made up by your selection from a number of optional modules that your institution makes available. The following are indicative of the types of option that are commonly available to study:

Law of evidence	Sports law	Tax law
Jurisprudence	Public international law	Family law
Child law	Dissertation	Media law
Employment law	Human rights law	Medical law
Company law	Business law	Environmental law

The options that are available in your institution will depend on a number of factors, including the research and teaching interests of the staff and the law school's view of what options should be made available to students.

As well as law options, it may well be the case that you can study some non-law subjects. It is common, for instance, for students to be given the opportunity to take a business or a foreign language module.

1.2.1.1 Choosing options

There may be some restrictions on which options you can take – it may be that you are permitted to take some options only in a particular year of your degree, or that you can only take a particular option if you have previously passed another. It may be that, because of timetabling issues, some options cannot be taken together (for example, you may not be able to take both sports law and tax law).

That aside, the following factors may inform your choice of module; each of them, I believe, is a rational consideration:

- *Assessment*: Students may choose options based on the method by which the different modules are assessed. So, a student with a dislike of examinations may try to choose options that are not assessed in this way.
- *Enjoyment and interest*: Students are more likely to do well in subjects in which they have a genuine interest and that they believe they will enjoy.
- *Further study*: Students who plan to go on to further study, say to undertake a masters degree or doctorate, may choose their options with that in mind. So, they may choose subjects that they intend to study in depth as a postgraduate student. Students who want to undertake a research degree may decide that it will be useful to gain experience researching and writing a substantial project and may, therefore, choose to undertake a dissertation. I discuss various options for further study, including the difference between taught and research degrees, in Chapter 11.
- *Future career*: Students may choose options on the basis of their future career aspirations. For example, those who wish to specialise in corporate law may choose options that reflect that. I should note that, in one sense, it is not necessary to study the area of law in which you wish to practise; you will be able to develop the requisite expertise in the later parts of your training or when you enter into the profession. However, taking a module in the area of law in which you wish to practise may demonstrate to a future employer your commitment to that specialism.
- *The lecturer teaching the subject*: Students often choose to take, or not to take, a module because of their feelings about the lecturer they believe is going to teach it. This is understandable. It is the way of the world that, for individual students, some lecturers are simply more engaging teachers, more likable or more able to convey their subject than others. Moreover, if you like

❝❞	LECTURERS' THOUGHTS
Anna	'The received wisdom is that students shouldn't consider whether they like a tutor or not when they choose their options. I disagree with that. At the end of the day, we are all just people, and it's only natural to take to some people more than others. If there is a tutor that you simply can't take to, for whatever reason, then you're unlikely to do well in their subject.'

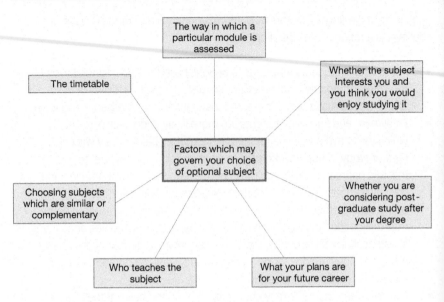

Figure 1.2 Factors governing choice of optional subjects

the way a class is taught, you are more likely to enjoy and be interested in the subject and, consequently, do well. It is worth remembering, though, that there is no guarantee that the person who has taught a subject in the past will continue to do so: for a variety of reasons, staff leave or change their role.

- *Choosing subjects because they are similar or complementary*: It may be that you choose subjects that are alike, or that complement each other. This might be because of your career or postgraduate plans or simply because you are interested in the general area in question. So, for example, you may choose to study a number of related international law options because this reflects your interest or career ambitions.
- *The timetable*: It may be that you are restricted in your choice of module because of the time or day on which it is taught. It may be, for example, that you would love to take jurisprudence, but that the lecture takes place at a time when you have an alternative commitment that you cannot escape.

When deciding on which options you should study, you might find it useful to talk to students, perhaps in other years, who have taken the modules you are interested in. You might also find it useful to talk to the lecturer who usually delivers the module.

1.2.2   **Combined degrees**

Institutions will often offer combined qualifying law degrees, where you study law in combination with another subject. There are numerous possible subjects with which the study of law may be combined; some common examples are:

- law with business;
- law with criminology;
- law with French (or another modern language);
- law with politics.

Such combined degrees will be attractive to those who want to obtain a qualifying law degree and also study another subject in addition to law.

Undertaking such degrees will, though, reduce the number of optional subjects that you may take. The reason for this is that you have to study a sufficient amount of law on the degree for it to be a qualifying law degree and a sufficient amount of the secondary subject in order for it to be a law with that second subject degree; this means that there is less space in your degree for optional choices.

1.3   **DIFFERENT STAFF**

There are various people involved in the delivery of your degree and they have different and, often, multiple roles. In this section, I want to introduce you to some of the more common roles that you will encounter or hear about.

Lecturer, senior lecturer, principal lecturer, reader and professor

The differences among these types of lecturer will vary across institutions and, in fact, some institutions may not use these titles at all. In some countries, it is the case that all lecturers at higher-education level are given the title 'professor' (though there will be levels of seniority between professors). In the UK, this is not common: in most UK institutions, a professor has a particular role, and other titles are used for those who are lecturers but not professors.

The difference between the categories of lecturer, senior lecturer and principal lecturer is one of seniority and, usually, experience – a senior lecturer will be more senior, have more responsibility and (usually) be more experienced than a lecturer.

Readers and professors will usually be lecturers who have significant research experience and are expected to undertake a research role and provide research leadership within their institution. In some institutions, readers will be known as associate professors.

Programme leader

In different institutions, programme leaders may alternatively be known as programme convenors or co-ordinators. They are usually one of the lecturers teaching the degree.

Although the function of programme leaders will differ from institution to institution, their central role is an oversight one: to co-ordinate the delivery of the degree and to ensure that it runs as well as possible. To this end, they will be responsible for making certain:

- that the degree programme is academically coherent;
- that the programme is academically rigorous, and that the manner in which students are assessed is appropriate;
- that the degree is delivered in such a way that it enables all students to attain their full potential; and
- that any concerns raised by the external examiner are adequately addressed. (The role of external examiners is considered below.)

Module leaders

Module leaders may also be known as module convenors. They are responsible for the delivery of a particular module and will lead the other lecturers who may teach on it. The role of module leaders will usually include:

- organising the module to make sure that it is effectively taught;
- making certain that students know what is expected of them in terms of attendance and assessment;
- deciding the content of the module (what topics will be taught), how it will be assessed, and what the recommended text for that module is (i.e. what textbook will be recommended to students for purchase); he or she may make these choices in consultation with other staff, but, ultimately, it will be the module leader who is responsible; and
- ensuring that student assessments are marked consistently and at the correct standard, and that students have adequate opportunity to receive feedback on their assessment performance.

First and second markers

For all assessments, there will be a first and a second marker. The first marker will mark the individual assessments of students; on modules that are delivered by more than one tutor, the first marking will be shared among those who teach the module. The role of the second marker is to ensure that the first markers are marking at the correct standard. This will usually involve the second marker looking at a sample of the assessments (exam papers or coursework) from each grade bracket (firsts, 2:1s, fails, etc.); on some modules, however, the second marker may look at all the assessments (particularly where a small number of students are taking a particular module).

External examiners

External examiners are established, experienced academics from another institution – i.e. they are external to the institution for which they are an external examiner.

The role of external examiners is one of quality assurance: to confirm that students on particular modules – or, sometimes, across the whole degree – are being assessed appropriately, and that the marks awarded by the lecturers are correct – that they are not too high or too low.

1.4   DEGREE CLASSIFICATIONS AND GRADE BOUNDARIES

Most readers will be aware of the different degree classifications that UK universities award. They are:

- first-class degrees (first);
- upper second-class degrees (2:1);
- lower second-class degrees (2:2);
- third-class degrees (third);
- ordinary degrees.

For first-class, 2:1, 2:2 and third-class law degrees, the recipients will have an honours degree, which allows them to place the abbreviation 'Hons' in brackets following LLB after their name. For example:

Larry Lawyer LLB (Hons)

The ordinary degree is a non-honours degree. It is typically awarded where a student has failed to pass or complete some aspects of the degree.

To explain a little further: an honours degree is awarded where a student has completed modules amounting to 360 credits of study, and an ordinary degree is usually awarded where a student has completed modules amounting to at least 300 credits. Each of your modules will be worth a certain number of credits, and this is calculated on the basis that each credit is assumed to amount to 10 hours' worth of study; e.g. a 20-credit module is assumed to require 200 hours' worth of study.

I should note that slightly different rules apply in Scotland, where it is commonly the case that an ordinary degree is achieved after three years as an undergraduate, and an honours degree after four.

The degree classification (whether one receives a first, 2:1, etc.) is usually based on a calculation of the marks obtained in the second and third year of a full-time degree (or the equivalent of a part-time degree). In essence, the calculation will be an average of all the second- and third-year marks. Actually, it is a little more complicated than that sounds, because the calculation has to take into account some other variables, such as the credit weighting of the modules taken. Also, the regulations of some institutions require that the lowest mark received in the second and third year be discounted when the classification is calculated. Moreover, in some institutions, greater weight is given to third-year marks than second-year marks – this is colloquially known as exit velocity.

Although the actual calculation of your classification may be complicated, in most cases one can assume that, if the majority of a student's marks are, say, in the 2:1 bracket, then they will be awarded a 2:1 degree.

Grade boundaries

Most UK universities set the boundaries between the different grade brackets as follows:

- first class (first): 70 per cent or higher;
- upper-second class (2:1): 60–69 per cent;
- lower-second class (2:2): 50–59 per cent;
- third class (third): 40–49 per cent;
- fail: 39 per cent or below.

1.5   UNDERSTANDING THE ROLE OF, AND GETTING THE MOST FROM, YOUR LECTURERS

Your lecturers will be very busy people. Their role is multifaceted, and only a portion of it involves dealing directly with undergraduate students. As well as teaching you, the role of your lecturers is likely to include the following:

- *Teaching other undergraduate and postgraduate students*: Your lecturers will teach a variety of students in the law school and, perhaps, in other departments in your institution (e.g. they may teach media law to journalism students or business law to business students).
- *Supervising the dissertations of undergraduate and postgraduate students*: It is likely that your lecturers will be supervising the dissertation work of undergraduate students and, often, postgraduate students taking a masters degree or a doctorate.
- *Marking the work of students*: Marking students' work is one of the most important functions lecturers undertake, and it is very time consuming.
- *Engaging in research*: Many of your lecturers will also be expected to engage in research as part of their role.
- *Attending conferences*: Lecturers will often be away from the university attending research or teaching conferences, both in their own country and abroad.
- *Consultation*: Your lecturers may be using their expertise and knowledge to advise external bodies (i.e. bodies outside your institution). It is not uncommon, for instance, for lecturers to be engaged by national or international governmental bodies.
- *Administrative duties*: Your lecturers will have a number of administrative duties, both within the law school and across your institution. These might be acting as programme or module leaders – with all the administrative work entailed in those roles (see Section 1.3 above for a brief account of these roles) – and might also include sitting on, or even chairing, various committees involved in ensuring the smooth running of your law school and the institution.
- *Acting as external examiner at another institution*: I gave a brief description of the function of external examiners in Section 1.3, above. External examiners are an essential part of higher education – ensuring that standards across different institutions are broadly equivalent – and many of your lecturers will be external examiners at other institutions.

So, you will see that your lecturers are unlikely to be dealing only with you and your classmates; they will be involved in many other things. Moreover, being a lecturer is a job, and your lecturers will have a life, family and interests outside work. That is, although your lecturers will be dedicated and hard-working, they need – and are entitled – to have time for themselves and their families, which includes free time at weekends and evenings and taking annual leave.

Recognising these facts will help you to understand the best way to contact, arrange to meet and get help from your lecturers.

1.5.1   Contacting, arranging to meet and getting help from your lecturers

As it happens, as I write this, I have just returned from two weeks' annual leave during which I holidayed with my family. Prior to that, I had some work commitments away from my institution. This means that I had not physically been in my office for almost three weeks. On my return to the office, there was a message on my phone that had been left by a student two weeks earlier. Fortunately, the matter was not important, but this illustrates the issue: lecturers, because of the nature of their role, may be absent from their office for long periods of time.

Given this, generally, the best way to contact your lecturers is by email. This is because, among other things, your lecturers can access and respond to emails while they are away from the office. In addition, if you contact by email, your lecturers are able to carefully consider what you are asking and their response.

Of course, that does not preclude you from telephoning or simply calling in to see them. In fact, your lecturers will usually provide some specific times when they will be in their office to see students who simply want to drop in. But, mostly, the best way to contact your lecturers is by email.

In a wholly unscientific survey, I asked four of my colleagues how they prefer to be contacted by students and why. As you will see, each of them mentioned email as a preference or as the most useful for the students.

Arranging to meet your lecturers

If you are attempting to arrange a meeting with your lecturers, try to be as flexible as you can. Your tutors will appreciate that, like them, you may also have other commitments outside your degree. However, it is little use sending your lecturer an email saying, in effect: 'I would like to meet you and the only time I have

> ## LECTURERS' THOUGHTS
>
> ### How do you prefer to be contacted by students, and why?

Anna	'[I prefer] email because, as a lecturer, you are an incredibly busy person, sometimes dealing with a lot of students, and it's easy to forget what you've been asked. With email, there's a written record of what the student actually wants. Also, lecturers set aside time to deal with emails, so you're more likely to get a good response.'
Graham	'Email – [it is] easier to keep a record, and the student has a record of the response.'
Heather	'Face to face after lectures when it relates to something in the lecture, but if it's to do with submission dates, explaining absence or to arrange a meeting, then email.'
David	'I do not really have a preferred method. What I do say is, if the query relates to, say, their work, research or thoughts or concerns about coursework or an exam, I always suggest that they contact me by email, [not least] because it encourages them to formulate their concerns and enables me to respond more directly than I could orally; [it also] means that they have a record of my response that they can reread and reflect upon and that might be lost in an oral conversation.'

available is Friday at 2 p.m.'. It should be obvious that your lecturer may not be able to meet at the time you specify. Moreover, any lack of flexibility from you may be reciprocated; for instance, they might reply: 'Sorry, I can only meet on Monday at 9 a.m.'.

When trying to arrange a meeting, offer your tutor a number of options. So, for instance, Figure 1.3 shows what you might write.

Interacting with your lecturers

Broadly speaking, when dealing with your lecturers (and, indeed, with other members of staff and your fellow students), you should adopt a friendly and courteous approach. You should be respectful, treating them as you would want to be treated, without being obsequious (toadying and overly deferential).

To: Leonard Lecturer
From: Samantha Student
Subject: Meeting

Dear Leonard

Would it be possible to arrange to meet you this week or next to get some feedback on my Property law exam?

I work on Wednesday afternoons and am in classes on Monday mornings, Tuesdays between 9 and 11am, and Friday afternoons; other than that, I am free to meet at a time that suits you.

Thanks and best wishes

Samantha

Figure 1.3 Suggested email requesting a meeting

It will usually be the case that your lecturers prefer you to call them by their first name. If, however, they make it clear that they would like something more formal, then you should comply.

Taking a relatively informal but polite approach is appropriate, primarily for three reasons:

1   It is appropriate to behave toward other people with courtesy and respect – it is simply the right thing to do.
2   It is the professional way to behave, and acting in this way as a student will mean that you are accustomed to acting in the correct manner when you enter your chosen career.

WORK SMARTER

Treating your lecturers, other staff and fellow students with courtesy and respect is not just the right thing to do, it is also the smart thing to do – you may need the help of your tutors or the others around you at some point and it is more likely to be forthcoming if you treat them decently.

3   Throughout your degree, and after, you may need the help of your lecturers. For example, you may need them to take the time to explain something you are finding difficult, to provide support because some unexpected issue has arisen that disrupts your studies or to provide a potential employer with a reference for you. You are more likely to receive this help if you have acted courteously.

When emailing lecturers, there is no need to be deferential or overly formal. Similarly, you should not be too informal. Also:

- do not use text speak in emails – your message should be in clear English, so that the recipient can make sense of it;
- do not end your email with kisses;
- if it is not clear from your email address who you are, make it clear in your email, for instance, by signing your full name; your first name alone may not be sufficient – remember, your lecturers may be dealing with a number of students who share your first name; and
- if your private email address may be considered embarrassing or offensive, use a different one or your institutional email account.

1.6   EXTRACURRICULAR ACTIVITIES

For many students, higher education is not simply about getting a qualification; it is also about developing as a person and broadening interests and horizons.

Your law school, and perhaps your institution, will most likely have different clubs or societies that you can join and activities in which you can engage. So, for example, it is likely that you will be able to:

- join the student law society of your institution;
- engage in mooting competitions (see Section 8.2 of Chapter 8 for more information about mooting);
- attend lectures given by visiting speakers, including practising lawyers, judges and academics from other institutions;
- attend events with the law school's alumni (past students); and
- have the opportunity to go on a visit organised by your law school, for instance, to visit some of the institutions associated with the European Union and the European Convention on Human Rights.

A little too informal

To:	Terence Tutor
From:	Penelope Pupil
Subject:	Promissory estoppel and this week's lecture

Hey

I'd rly luv it if u'd tell us abt tht promissory estoppel thing agn this wk

Luv

Pen xxxx

A little too formal and obsequious

To:	Terence Tutor
From:	Penelope Pupil
Subject:	Promissory estoppel and this week's lecture

Dear Dr Tutor

I hope you are well on this fine morning and do not mind me disturbing your peace with this enquiry. I do not want to inconvenience you or put you to too much trouble but I have been struggling to understand the concept of promissory estoppel and I would be exceedingly grateful if you could take some time in this week's lecture to reappraise my fellow students and me of the basics.

Yours sincerely

Penelope Pupil (Ms)

Probably just right

To:	Terence Tutor
From:	Penelope Pupil
Subject:	Promissory estoppel and this week's lecture

Dear Terence

If you get a chance, would you mind going over promissory estoppel again in this week's contract lecture – I've been reading over it in the recommended text and I'm struggling to fully understand it

Thanks and best wishes

Penny

Figure 1.4 Emails of varying levels of formality

Of course, you may find the opportunity to join the different societies or engage in the various extracurricular activities enjoyable in itself. In addition, participating in different institutional events or organisations will enable you to develop a network of contacts among students in your own year, in different years and perhaps on different degrees. This, in itself, may be valuable, and it may also provide you with a greater sense of belonging. Further, it is always useful to have friends and contacts beyond those with whom you normally study, because they may be able to give you help or advice that would be otherwise unavailable to you.

It may also be the case that, with some events – for instance, visiting speaker or alumni events – there will be a possibility for you to make valuable contacts with, say, practitioners, which may, in turn, lead to work placement opportunities (see Chapter 11 for an explanation of the benefits of work experience).

Engaging with various societies and in extracurricular activities may also make you more attractive to a future potential employer. Being an active member of your student law society, for example, is something you can put on your CV and will present you as a rounded and experienced individual with good social and interpersonal skills – these are characteristics that many employers positively value and want to see.

Chapter 2
Getting the most out of your classes

In this chapter, I will:

- introduce the two main types of class used to teach undergraduate law students: lectures and seminars;
- consider the importance of attending all classes;
- discuss the behaviour expected of students in class;
- look at how you can best prepare for, and take notes during, lectures and how you may best reinforce your recall and understanding afterwards;
- discuss the importance of preparing for, and participating in, seminars.

2.1 INTRODUCTION

Broadly speaking, your degree will be delivered via two types of class – lectures and seminars – and, as Table 2.1 indicates, there are some significant differences between them.

Lectures and seminars are obviously related: usually the lecture will introduce a subject that will be explored in more depth and detail in a later seminar.

2.2 THE IMPORTANCE OF ATTENDANCE

It is difficult to over-emphasise how important it is for you to attend all classes. Indeed, almost all lecturers will tell you that there is a direct correlation between how well a student does and their attendance record – those whose attendance is poor usually perform badly.

Table 2.1 Lectures and seminars

	Lectures	Seminars
Size	Lectures are large group sessions, and, in some institutions, in foundational or popular modules, it is not unusual to find yourself in a class of 200 or more students	Seminars are small group sessions. You will usually find yourself in a class of about 12, sometimes a little more, sometimes fewer
Purpose	The purpose of a lecture is to give you a broad, general introduction to the subject matter in question	Seminars are usually designed to allow you to examine the subject in a little more depth, to clarify your understanding and to consider points that your lecturer considers important or that students often find difficult
Delivery	Usually, in lectures, the lecturer plays the main role, delivering the class to the students. There may be some interaction – for instance, the lecturer may ask questions of you, ask you to take a moment to discuss something or permit you to ask questions – but, in the main, the lecturer does the majority of the speaking	Seminars are interactive, and students are required to contribute to the discussion and to answer questions. The lecturer will clarify some things, but seminars are not mini lectures, and your lecturer will require students in the seminar to do a significant amount of the talking
Preparation	As I state below, it is a good idea to undertake some preparatory reading before the lecture, and, in fact, the lecturer may require you to do so	You will be required to undertake a significant amount of preparation before a seminar, which will likely include: – reading specified parts of your textbook and other secondary materials; – reading cases and legislative provisions; and – preparing answers to questions set by the lecturer

In fact, if you fail to attend, you may not receive the broad introduction to the subject matter of the class as provided in lectures, or the in-depth consideration of it that takes place in seminars, and you may find it difficult to make up for this by your own reading.

In addition, a failure to attend will mean that you will not develop an appreciation of whether you are working at the appropriate level. Every year, lecturers in all institutions receive emails from students whose attendance has been poor, writing, in effect, that they apologise for their lack of attendance but that it is 'ok', because they have been 'keeping up with the work'. Such students may think they are 'keeping up with the work', but they will not know whether they are developing sufficient depth of understanding because this would only be apparent through attendance at, and engagement in, class.

COMMON ERROR

Persistently absent students often justify their absence by claiming that they are 'keeping up with the work'. While this might be true, a failure to attend classes will mean that they do not receive explicit and implicit feedback about whether they are developing the appropriate level of understanding.

Moreover, for all modules, your lecturer will examine some things in more depth than another lecturer would have done, and may not consider some aspects of the subject at all. What is covered will reflect your lecturer's interests and view about what they consider important, and these things may also be reflected in the assessments you have to undertake for that module. If you fail to attend, you will not become familiar with the emphases the lecturer gives to some aspects of the subject, and this may affect your assessment performance. Indeed, lecturers sometimes will provide advice in class about how to answer the assessment for that module. If you do not attend, you will not receive this advice.

You should also remember that, wherever you go after your degree – whether employment, further study, or to undertake the practical training to become a lawyer – your lecturers will be required to provide a reference for you and will be specifically asked to comment on your attendance. If your attendance at classes has been poor, they will be obliged to state this, which may harm your future plans.

Furthermore, your acceptance on to a degree will be a contractual agreement with your institution, and this agreement may contain an explicit or implicit requirement of attendance. If you fail to attend, you may find that you are withdrawn as a student. Indeed, some institutions have an attendance requirement that is linked to the marks you receive, so that, for instance, if your attendance drops below a certain figure (say 75 per cent of classes) then your mark for that particular module is capped (restricted).

WORK SMARTER

Attending all your classes is probably the single most important thing you can do to improve your chances of getting good grades.

Of course, some absences are unavoidable because of, say, sickness or other emergency. Where this is the case, you should:

- contact the relevant lecturer to apologise for, and explain, your absence;
- ask whether there is an alternative that you can attend, if you have missed a seminar;
- ask the relevant lecturer whether you can book some time with them, if you have missed a lecture, so that they can give you an outline of what you have missed; if you do this, you should make sure that you prepare beforehand by reading the relevant parts of your textbook.

2.3   BEHAVIOUR IN CLASS

Your behaviour throughout the whole of your degree should be governed by the principles of courtesy and consideration – both to your lecturers and your fellow students.

In lectures, you should remember that your lecturers are giving a performance – not always an easy task in itself – and probably trying to achieve a number of difficult things at the same time: remember what they have to say and when, maintain some discipline in the class, make sure that their lecture is not too long or too short and keep students engaged and interested. Given this, you should not act in a way that is likely to break your lecturer's concentration or the flow of their thoughts.

You should, therefore, do the following:

- Make sure that you punctually attend all classes. This is because your late arrival might disturb the lecturer or other students. It may also mean that you miss something vital – the lecturer may spend the first ten minutes of a particular class giving some advice about, for instance, how to answer the coursework question for that module. Besides, remember that your lecturers may be asked by a future potential employer to provide a reference for you, and such requests always ask the referee to comment on the student's punctuality.
- Do not talk excessively during the lecture – you will disturb the lecturer and your fellow students.
- Do not use your mobile phone during the class, either to send texts or for anything else. Indeed, your phone should be switched off, or at least switched to silent and placed out of view in your pocket or bag. If you do need to keep your phone to hand because, say, you are expecting an emergency call, inform the lecturer of this before the class starts.
- Do not use your phone, laptop computer or other device to play games or update your social network page during the lecture. It is incredibly discourteous towards the lecturer and may distract other students.

LECTURERS' PET HATES

'I take it as a personal insult if I see students using their mobile phones in class or on Facebook or Twitter. I just think, what is the point of you being here if you are not going to take notice?'

Almost all institutions will have rules governing how you should behave in class, and, if you do not behave appropriately, you may find that you are asked to leave, which may be embarrassing for you and may affect your ability to do well in that module.

2.4 LECTURES

As mentioned above, lectures are large group-teaching sessions where the lecturer, for the most part, delivers the material, though some lecturers may take a more interactive, two-way approach.

The way in which individual lectures are delivered will change from lecturer to lecturer and will depend on their personality and how they believe they can best help students to understand. So, for instance, some lecturers will provide detailed handouts, whereas others may not, and some will use presentation software, whereas others will simply speak. You will find that you quickly adapt to the individual style and teaching method employed by different lecturers.

Before the lecture

One of the best pieces of advice I can give you is for you to undertake some reading before the lecture. Doing this will give you some prior knowledge of the subject matter of the lecture, which will help you to maintain your attention during it and even help you get back on track if your mind wanders for a moment. Engaging in prior reading will also provide you with sufficient information to help you better understand and engage with the class; this is true even if you do not completely understand your pre-lecture reading.

You may, therefore, find it helpful to:

- read the lecture handout beforehand if possible; this will give you an indication of the structure of, and the main points and cases that will be discussed in, the class;
- read the relevant chapter of one of the simpler, more accessible types of textbook. These will be brief and basic enough to provide you with a good introduction to the basics (see Section 3.5 of Chapter 3 for an introduction to the different levels of textbook available);
- read the relevant chapter of the recommended textbook for that module; even if you simply skim-read the chapter, you will be giving yourself a decent base understanding that you will further develop in the lecture.

TIP BOX

It will be useful to read the relevant chapter, or chapters, of one of the simpler, more accessible textbooks before a lecture so that you have some prior knowledge of the subject matter which will, in turn, help you better understand and engage with the class.

When attending the lecture, you should arrive in good time and sit where you can comfortably hear and see and from where you can easily ask questions.

LECTURERS' PET HATES

'My biggest pet hate with regard to lectures is students arriving late.'

Taking notes during the lecture

There is no one technique for taking notes. Rather, you should adopt a method that works for you. Some people like to take fairly detailed notes; others take a more basic approach. Some take linear notes, whereas others use a spider diagram or similar diagrammatic approach (see Section 6.4.2 of Chapter 6 for an example of a spider diagram used in planning coursework). Some use a pen and paper, and others use a laptop or similar electronic device.

Whichever method you adopt:

- remember to take your pen and paper or laptop with you to the class;
- do not try to capture everything said; if you do, you may not devote sufficient attention to listening and comprehending what is communicated; on the other hand, your notes should not be so sparse that you will not be able to make sense of them later;
- if using paper, use an A4 notebook rather than a small one and leave enough space so that you can make additions or clarifications to your notes after the lecture;
- date and title your notes and number all the pages you use; this will be useful for future reference or if your notes become disorganised;
- where you can, use abbreviations and shorthand, rather than writing out in full; for example:
  - PM – prime minister
  - Gov – government
  - RoL – rule of law
  - O&A – offer and acceptance
  - Cons – consideration
  - Neg – negligence
  - AR and MR – *actus reus* and *mens rea*.

Recording lectures

You may find it beneficial to make an audio recording of lectures. Doing so might help you to clarify your lecture notes after the class. If you do wish to record the lecture:

- Ask the permission of each individual lecturer and remember that they may well refuse.
- Do not rely solely on your recording; you may find that it has not captured what was said as well as you would hope. Make sure that you take adequate written notes as well.
- After the lecture, do not spend an inordinate amount of time listening to, or transcribing, the recording – it will probably add little to your understanding, and your time can be better employed.

LECTURERS' PET HATES

'I'll tell you what is a pet hate – people recording me without permission.'

After the lecture

If possible, you should read the notes you have taken in the lecture within an hour or so of the end of the class. This will:

- reinforce your recollection of what the lecturer said while your memory is still relatively fresh;
- enable you to make additions to your notes – again, while your memory is still fresh – to clarify points so that they are clearer for later use, when you are revising or preparing for seminars;
- allow you to identify things that you do not sufficiently understand and that you can then attempt to clarify with further reading or in the seminar.

You should also try to read the relevant chapter of your textbook within a day or two of the lecture. This, again, will reinforce your recollection and understanding of the subject matter of the class. It will also probably provide you with a slightly different point of view from that of your lecturer, and this will help you develop a more rounded and sophisticated understanding.

WORK SMARTER

Try to read your lecture notes within an hour or so of the end of the lecture and the relevant pages of your textbook within a day or two after the class. This will reinforce your memory of the lecture, aid your understanding and make it easier to recall the information when you need it.

2.5   SEMINARS

Before the seminar

You will be expected to do a significant amount of preparation for each seminar you attend. You may be asked to:

- read particular pages of the recommended textbook, journal articles, cases and legislation; and
- prepare answers to questions that your lecturer will use as the basis for discussion in the seminar.

LECTURERS' THOUGHTS

Anna	'Seminars are the place where students are supposed to develop and progress towards being a graduate, and that doesn't happen by magic without them doing the preparation and the work.'

Figure 2.1 shows a typical example of the preparation required for a seminar.

You *must* undertake all the reading required of you, in full, and prepare answers to all the questions well in advance of the class. If you do not:

- Your lecturer will soon know, and you may find yourself in a very uncomfortable position. In fact, it is not uncommon for lecturers to ask students to leave a class if it becomes obvious that they have failed to do the preparation required of them.

JUDICIAL REVIEW 3: PROCEDURAL IMPROPRIETY, REMEDIES AND OUSTER CLAUSES

Reading:
Elliott, M. & Thomas, R., (2014) Public Law, 2nd Edn., OUP, chapter 12 and pages 509-511 and 529-535

Cases:
R v North and East Devon Health Authority, ex parte Coughlan [2001] QB 213
Dimes v Grand Junction Canal Proprietors (1852) 3 HL Cas 759
Porter v Magill [2002] 2 AC 357
Anisminic v Foreign Compensation Commission [1969] 2 AC 147

Questions:

1.   What is meant by procedural impropriety?

2.   What are the two rules of natural justice?

3.   Briefly explain how a legitimate expectation may arise.

4.   Explain the rules against bias.

5.   Explain what an ouster clause is. What is the courts' usual approach to such clauses?

6.   Prepare an answer for the following question:

The (fictitious) Law Lecturers Act 2005 establishes a scheme of compensation for law lecturers traumatised by years of teaching unruly students. The Act gives the Secretary of State for Education the power to decide when the scheme should take effect; section 5 of the Act, which gives the Secretary of State this power, reads:

> "Section 5
> (1)   Given the importance of the decision, it shall be for the Secretary of State to decide when the compensation scheme shall take effect.
> (2)   In reaching the decision in subsection (1), the Secretary of State shall take into account representations from interested parties."

On 1 March 2006, the Secretary of State issues a press release stating that he will only take into account representations which are accompanied by a £500 administration fee. He also states that, regardless of any representations, he will not, under any circumstances, bring the scheme into effect for at least two years.

On 6 March 2006, he writes to the Institute of Law Lecturers (ILL) inviting them to make representations as to when the scheme should take effect. The letter states that any representations must reach the Department of Education by 10 March 2006.

On 13 March 2006, the Secretary of State issues another press release announcing the establishment of a Compensation Committee which will decide when the scheme is to take effect. In August 2006, the Committee announces that the scheme will not be brought into being at all.

Advise the Institute of Law Lecturers who wish to challenge this decision and the way that it has been made.

Figure 2.1 Example of seminar questions and reading

- You will not be able to contribute to the discussion in the seminar in an intelligent way.
- You will not get as much from the class in terms of developing your understanding as you would if you had adequately prepared.

LECTURERS' PET HATES

'[A pet hate of mine is] students who just turn up for seminars and do no preparation whatsoever [beforehand] and think that it is acceptable to simply sit and write down what everyone else is saying.'

You will also find it useful to read the relevant lecture notes in preparation for the seminar and you may find it worthwhile to engage in other reading beyond that which you have been asked to do.

LECTURERS' THOUGHTS

| Graham | 'In seminars, I like students to go beyond the core reading and to have done their own further research.' |

As part of your preparation, ensure that you are able to give an account of all that you have read. In particular, you should be able to:

- describe the facts, decision and relevance of any case that you have been asked to read (see Chapter 3 for advice about reading cases);
- give a brief summary of the argument made in any journal article that you are required to read (see Section 3.6 of Chapter 3 for advice about reading journal articles).

During the seminar

- Ensure that you make an effort to contribute to the discussion in the class. Sometimes, students do not like to speak because they are afraid they may say something that is incorrect. Try not to worry about this; remember, seminars are a learning forum, and being wrong – and having your mistakes corrected – is an inherent part of learning. Moreover, your lecturer will be sympathetic if you have tried to understand but have had some difficulty. In fact, they will be more understanding of your making an incorrect contribution than if you fail to contribute at all.

- Be considerate to your fellow students. Treat them, and their views, with courtesy and respect. Allow other people to speak and do not interrupt or talk over other people.
- If you have not understood something, either while preparing for, or during, the seminar, do not hesitate to ask your lecturer to clarify.

Chapter 3
Reading and independent study

This chapter will:

- discuss the importance of reading and independent study;
- introduce you to the difference between primary and secondary materials;
- provide a brief description of textbooks, cases and materials books, journal articles, case comments, monographs and edited collections;
- give advice about reading and understanding cases;
- explain the difference between primary and secondary legislation and explain the main features of Acts of Parliament;
- provide advice about reading and understanding textbooks, journal articles and chapters from edited collections;
- give the meaning and usage of Latin terms that are commonly employed in legal and academic writing.

3.1 INTRODUCTION

University Challenge, the television quiz show, has been on our screens since 1962 (with a short break between 1987 and 1994). In the old days, and sometimes now, the contestants would introduce themselves by saying that they were 'reading' a particular subject. For example: 'Hi, I'm Tim from Bristol and I'm reading law'. This is because that is precisely what undergraduate students are supposed to do – to read. In fact, you should spend the vast majority of your time as a law student outside the classroom, engaged in reading various materials such as textbooks, law reports and journal articles. During term time, full-time law students will spend no more than about 10–15 hours a week in class (less, pro rata, for part-time students). The rest of the time should be spent in independent study – about 25–30 hours a week for full-time students. Indeed, as a law student, you will (or you should) probably do more reading than you have ever done before.

You may, therefore, think of your degree as a kind of guided learning: your lecturers are there to guide you, and to push you forward, but you undertake most of the work yourself. They provide the framework for your learning, but you are the one who develops your knowledge in depth. To be sure, often, the difference between a good and average student is the amount of independent study in which they engage.

TIP BOX

Often, the difference between a good and an average student turns on the amount of independent study in which they engage.

You will be expected to read a variety of materials, including:

- law reports
- textbooks
- journal articles.

Some of your reading will be directed or suggested by your lecturers, and some will be materials that you have found yourself. Where your lecturers require you to read something, you *must* read it, in full. Apart from anything else, it can be a very uncomfortable experience sitting in a classroom, trying to explain to one of your lecturers, in front of your fellow students, why you have ignored their instruction to read a particular article or the pages of a textbook.

You might be interested to know that it is probably one of the most common complaints of all lecturers (including this one) that students do not read enough. My colleagues in universities and higher-education institutions throughout the land continue to be amazed by students who find it difficult to spend more than an hour or so reading outside the classroom, but appear to believe that they are going to get an excellent degree and go on to a fantastic legal career. Remember, these things are probably within your grasp, but only if you are willing to put in the time and work.

LECTURERS' PET HATES

Students not engaging in sufficient independent study is probably one of the most common pet hates of lecturers.

Engaging in a significant amount of independent reading has a number of benefits:

- The more you read, the more you will develop the breadth, depth and sophistication of your understanding. This will particularly be the case if you read the views of a number of different commentators (academics and others), because you will be exposed to different points of view that will help you to develop your own, nuanced understanding.
- Reading will help you broaden your vocabulary considerably (when I was first a law student, I constantly had a dictionary at my side because of the number of words that I had not encountered before and did not understand; at the time, it seemed to me that judges took particular delight in using fairly obscure words in their judgments).
- You will understand the way lawyers and academics use language, how they phrase things, and – in this way – you will begin to speak, write and think like a lawyer.
- You will learn the way that judges and academics structure their arguments, and this will help you to learn how to structure yours and what does, and does not, work as a valid argument.

3.2   DIFFERENT READING MATERIALS

3.2.1   Primary and secondary materials

There is a difference between reading the law and reading about the law. When you directly read judgments or legislation, you are reading the law. When you read textbooks, journal articles or other commentary, you are reading about the law.

In legal study, those materials that are direct legal sources – such as case law judgments or legislation – are known as primary sources or materials. Those materials that are commentary, critique or explanatory of the law – textbooks, monographs, journal articles and the like – are known as secondary sources or materials.

The distinction between primary and secondary materials is important. This is because the former are statements of the law, should be treated as such in your writing and, where possible, should be referred to directly as definitive statements of what the law is. The latter are not sources of law in themselves, and you should not treat them or write about them as though they were.

Table 3.1 Primary and secondary materials

Primary materials	Secondary materials
Case law	Textbooks
Legislation	Monographs
	Journal articles
	Case comments

Students do not always adequately recognise this distinction and sometimes use secondary materials as though they were primary materials. So, for instance, a student might write about what amounts to consideration in the law of contract and, rather than reference case law directly, they might cite the pages in a textbook that discusses it. Or, students sometimes refer to, say, a case but, rather than provide the citation in a footnote, they will refer to a secondary source that mentions it.

LECTURERS' PET HATES

'One of my pet hates, and a surprising number of students do it, is when a student references a textbook instead of the primary source.'

Of course, there is nothing wrong with informing your work with, and making reference to, secondary sources. Indeed, you should draw on a variety of appropriate primary and secondary materials when writing and developing your understanding. The error is when students refer to secondary materials as if they were sources of law in themselves.

3.2.2   Secondary materials

There are numerous secondary materials you can use to develop your understanding and in your coursework. This section will give you a brief description of some of the commonest.

Correct – citing the primary source directly

> The case of *Donoghue v Stevenson*[1] makes it clear that, when determining whether a defendant incurs liability for their negligent act, the courts will make use of a number of principles. First, they will ask
>
> ---------------------------------
>
> [1.] [1932] AC 562

Incorrect – citing a secondary source rather than the primary

> The case of *Donoghue v Stevenson*[1] makes it clear that, when determining whether a defendant incurs liability for their negligent act, the courts will make use of a number of principles. First, they will ask
>
> ---------------------------------
>
> [1.] C Elliott and F Quinn (2003) *Tort Law*, 4th ed., Harlow: Pearson, p. 15.

Figure 3.1 Correct and incorrect citations

3.2.3 Finding secondary materials

It is relatively easy to find appropriate secondary materials to help develop your understanding and to use when completing coursework. For instance:

- Your lecturer will probably instruct you to, or suggest that you, read particular journal articles, pages in a textbook, edited collections and the like.
- Sometimes, textbook writers will provide a further reading list after each chapter.
- Textbooks and journal articles will make reference to other secondary sources that you can then access.
- Textbooks, and sometimes journal articles, will contain a bibliography of the sources the authors have relied on, and you might want to consult these to see if any appear to be useful.
- You can physically go to your institution's library and walk along the relevant subject shelves to see if any of the books might be useful to you. Alternatively, you can use the library's catalogue (which will almost certainly be available online) to try to find relevant texts.

Table 3.2 Secondary materials

Textbooks	The majority of textbooks are written for undergraduate students, though some of the more sophisticated ones will be used by academics, practising lawyers and even judges. Textbooks are primarily designed to explain the law – to simply state what the legal position is – though they will often also contain some critique of the law or, where it is unclear, some contention about what the law should be. For any particular subject, there will be numerous textbooks, of different levels of accessibility and complexity. It is likely that, for each of your modules, your lecturer will recommend that you purchase a particular textbook to which they will refer throughout the module
Cases and materials books	Cases and materials books are written for undergraduate law students. They contain brief summaries of the facts and decisions of the leading cases in a particular subject and, usually, relevant extracts from the judgments. They will also contain excerpts from appropriate texts, such as leading textbooks or journal articles. A good cases and materials book can be a very worthwhile purchase and can save you a lot of time and energy in helping you understand primary and secondary sources
Journal articles	Journal articles are usually written by academics and, sometimes, practising lawyers or judges. There are also some that are written by students (though you should be more careful in using these, as their quality may be significantly lower than those written by more experienced and established commentators). Journal articles are often written with academics and practitioners in mind and are, accordingly, pitched at quite an advanced level. Despite this, as an undergraduate student, you must make extensive use of journal articles. Journal articles may attempt to do different things, including: • critique a particular area of law; • make an argument about what the law should be taken to be; • make an argument about what the underlying theoretical rationale of an area of law should be taken to be; • explain a particular area of law

Table 3.2 continued

Case comments	Case comments are a particular type of journal article. They will contain an explanation and critique of the facts and decision of a particular case. They may also site the case in its wider context, explaining its relevance for, and how it changes, the existing legal position. Case comments can be very useful in helping students understand a particular case
Monographs	Monographs are books that are usually written by academics for other academics or (less commonly) practising lawyers. They are quite advanced pieces of work. Like journal articles, they may attempt to do any of a number of things, such as: critique an area of law; make theoretical arguments about the law; or, critique the arguments of others. As an undergraduate student, you may be advised by your lecturers to read particular pages of a monograph, or you may decide to make use of them yourself, particularly if you are undertaking a dissertation
Edited texts	Edited texts are books containing chapters – usually linked by a particular theme – written by different authors. These are collected and edited by an editor or editors. Sometimes, a particular author may publish and edit a collection of their own essays or journal articles. Like journal articles and monographs, they will normally be written at quite an advanced level

- It is almost certain that your institution will provide you with access to Westlaw, and you can use the journal search facility to try to find relevant journal articles.

3.3 READING CASES

Throughout your degree, you will be expected to read the leading cases in each particular subject. There are a number of advantages to this, not least:

- You access the primary source directly rather than relying on a secondary source (i.e. someone else's interpretation) to tell you what the law is.
- You will better understand the language and arguments that lawyers use when arguing cases.

However, there are also some downsides to reading cases, including:

- Some cases are very long and complicated.
- You will sometimes be asked to read a case where the pertinent point – the relevant point for your subject – is a relatively minor aspect of the case. As a first-year undergraduate, for my contract law module, I remember reading – at the instruction of my lecturers – very lengthy cases about shipping law that made (what seemed to me) merely passing reference to contractual law.
- Judges often seem to like the sound of their own voice, or the length of their own judgments, and sometimes seem to use twenty words where five would have been adequate.

Given this, it will be useful for you to have some techniques to help you understand cases and better to manage the reading load that they generate. First, though, I will give a brief introduction to law reports.

3.3.1   Law reports

In common law jurisdictions such as England and Wales, decisions of the senior courts create precedents that are binding on other courts. In other words, the decisions of the courts are themselves sources of law. Over the centuries, these decisions have been recorded in an increasingly accurate way in law reports. These commonly contain:

- a brief summary of the facts and main legal dispute of a case and of the decision; followed by
- the full judgment handed down by the judges who determined the case.

Historically, these law reports have been available only in hard-copy form (i.e. in physical volumes) in specialist law libraries, including in university libraries. However, the advent of the Internet has meant that electronic versions of these law reports are available online, predominantly via two legal databases: Westlaw and LexisNexis. It is almost certain that your institution will provide access to these databases, as well as training in their use.

There are hundreds of different law reports that are available both in hard copy and online. Some of the most common are:

- the All England Law Reports – abbreviated as All ER;
- the Appeal Cases Law Reports – abbreviated as AC;

- the Queen's Bench Law Reports – abbreviated as QB;
- the Weekly Law Reports – abbreviated as WLR.

There are also more specialised law reports, such as:

- the Business Law Reports – abbreviated as Bus LR;
- the Common Market Law Reports – abbreviated as CMLR;
- the Environmental Law Reports – abbreviated as Env LR;
- the Housing Law Reports – abbreviated as HLR.

The same case may be reported in more than one law report. So, for example, the famous negligence case – *Donoghue v Stevenson* – is reported in a number of different law reports, including:

- the Appeal Cases law report of 1932 at page 562, cited as [1932] AC 562;
- the 1932 volume of the Session Cases (House of Lords) law reports at page 31, cited as 1932 SC (HL) 31;
- the 1932 volume of the Scottish Law Times at page 317, cited as 1932 SLT 317;
- the 1932 volume of the Weekly Notes at page 139, cited as [1932] WN 139; and
- the 1932 volume of the All England Report Reprints at page 1, cited as [1932] All ER Rep 1.

Guidance about the meaning of legal abbreviations, or about how certain law reports should be abbreviated, can be found on the Cardiff Index to Legal Abbreviations: www.legalabbrevs.cardiff.ac.uk/site/index

Law reports commonly have the features shown in Figure 3.2, though different law reports have different features.

3.3.1.1 Neutral citations

Since 2001, cases in the House of Lords, Privy Council, Court of Appeal and Administrative Court have been given a neutral citation by the courts. This means that, whether or not the case is reported in a law report, it will be given a unique reference number by which it may be identified, and an official transcript of the judgment will usually be available online. This practice has now been extended to the Supreme Court and the rest of the High Court. In addition, each paragraph of the judgments of these courts will be numbered, which means that particular parts may be identified and referenced.

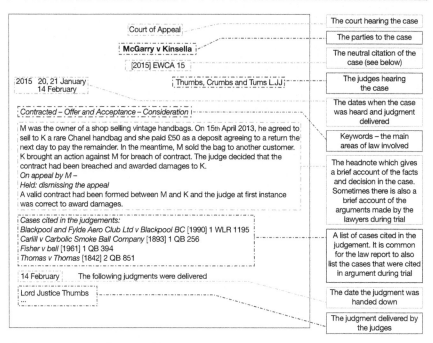

Figure 3.2 Common features of law reports

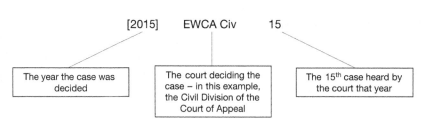

Figure 3.3 Neutral citation meaning

The neutral citation gives the date when the case is heard, which court heard it and the judgment number. So, in the fictional example of *McGarry v Kinsella* in Figure 3.2, the meaning of the neutral citation is as shown in Figure 3.3.

The neutral citations for the different courts are as shown in Table 3.3.

Table 3.3 Neutral citations for courts

UKSC	The Supreme Court
UKHL	The House of Lords
UKPC	The Privy Council
EWCA Civ	The Court of Appeal for England and Wales, Civil Division
EWCA Crim	The Court of Appeal for England and Wales, Criminal Division
EWHC	The High Court of England and Wales. There will also be an additional abbreviation indicating which division of the court heard the case or whether it was heard by the Administrative Court

3.3.2   Reading and understanding cases

As noted above, you will be required to read cases throughout your degree. For the most part, the cases you read will be those you have been asked to read by your lecturers. You may, though, find and read your own cases.

Your lecturers may tell you that you have to read all cases in full. I believe, however, that this is not always beneficial. Some cases are over a hundred pages in length, and it may be that only a small aspect of the judgment is relevant for you. In many situations, you will be working smarter if you read about the case and then read relevant parts of the judgment. You may be able to identify the relevant aspects of the judgment by:

- quickly skim-reading the judgment and pausing to read in depth those parts that you see are important;
- looking for the headnote of a law report, which will sometimes inform you which parts of the judgment deal with which aspects of the law;
- reading the judgment of the judge who is widely considered to have given the leading opinion (your textbooks might make this clear).

Having said that, there are benefits of sometimes reading a case in full, and you should consider doing so when:

- the case is an important one;
- the case is relatively short; or

- you are making detailed reference to the case in coursework or a dissertation and you need to ensure that what you write is accurate.

Whether reading a case in full or not, there are some practical steps that you can take to help you understand it.

Table 3.4 Practical steps you can take to help you understand the cases you read

You will often be reading a case for a particular purpose. For instance, you may have been asked to read a case in preparation for a seminar looking at the concept of consideration in your contract law module. Keep this in mind – that you are reading the case for a particular purpose – and make sure that you are able to do at least three things:

1 Be able to give a brief account of the facts of the case.
2 Be able to say what the decision in the case was (i.e. who won) and whether it was a unanimous or majority decision.
3 Most importantly, be able to say what the relevance of the case is for that particular class, coursework or whatever; i.e. why you have been asked to read that case.

Your textbook will often contain accounts of the facts and decisions of the most important cases in the subject, and you can use these as a stepping-stone to help you understand. Moreover, finding an account of a case in your textbook may help you understand its relevance to the particular area of law for which you have been asked to read it.

So, for example, imagine you have been asked to read *M v Home Office* [1994] 1 AC 377 for a seminar on the rule of law in your public law module. You can begin by looking at the table of cases in your textbook and finding the pages where the case is mentioned. Next, you can cross-reference these page numbers to the rule of law chapter (i.e. identify the pages where the case is mentioned that fall within the rule of law chapter), and reading the account of the case in this chapter should give you a good indication of why the case is relevant for that particular class.

Cases and materials books may also be used as stepping-stones to help you understand the facts, decision and relevance of a particular case. These will often give more details about a case and, for the more important cases, give relevant extracts from the judgments; they may even provide some additional explanation of these extracts and their significance.

Westlaw provides a case analysis facility that gives a brief account of the facts, decision and significance of the case. This is better for more recent cases than for older ones.

The headnote of the case in a law report is also helpful in aiding your understanding of the facts, decision and relevance of a case.

LECTURERS' THOUGHTS

Graham	'Sometimes in class, you see students with a printout from Westlaw of the facts [of a case] and abstract [i.e. summary] and they are unable to explain the case beyond this.'

WORK SMARTER

When attempting to understand a case, try to be able to answer the following three basic questions:

1. What are the facts of the case?
2. What was the decision and was it a unanimous or majority judgment?
3. Why is the case relevant for that particular class; why have you been asked to read it?

3.4   LEGISLATION

Unlike with case law, you are unlikely to be asked to read a full Act of Parliament or Statutory Instrument. Rather, you will be directed to read particular provisions of the legislation in question.

Generally speaking, legislation can be divided into two broad categories: primary legislation and secondary legislation.

Acts of Parliament will have the following features:

- *Short title*: this is the title that is usually used to refer to the Act.
- *Citation*: The citation will be the chapter number of the Act. In the fictional example in Figure 3.4, the Walking Dogs (Ormsborough Beach) Act was the

Table 3.5 Primary and secondary legislation

Primary legislation	Secondary legislation
Acts of Parliament (also known as statutes)	Statutory Instruments Orders in Council

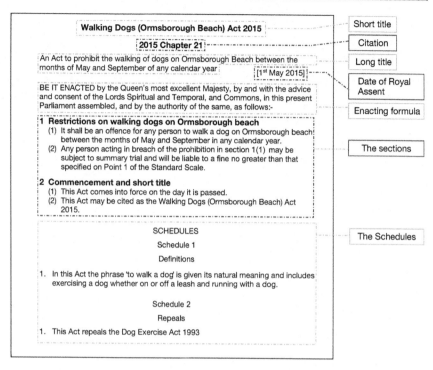

Walking Dogs (Ormsborough Beach) Act 2015	Short title
2015 Chapter 21	Citation
An Act to prohibit the walking of dogs on Ormsborough Beach between the months of May and September of any calendar year	Long title
[1st May 2015]	Date of Royal Assent
BE IT ENACTED by the Queen's most excellent Majesty, by and with the advice and consent of the Lords Spiritual and Temporal, and Commons, in this present Parliament assembled, and by the authority of the same, as follows:-	Enacting formula

1 Restrictions on walking dogs on Ormsborough beach

   (1) It shall be an offence for any person to walk a dog on Ormsborough beach between the months of May and September in any calendar year.

   (2) Any person acting in breach of the prohibition in section 1(1) may be subject to summary trial and will be liable to a fine no greater than that specified on Point 1 of the Standard Scale.

2 Commencement and short title

   (1) This Act comes into force on the day it is passed.

   (2) This Act may be cited as the Walking Dogs (Ormsborough Beach) Act 2015.

                              The sections

SCHEDULES

Schedule 1

Definitions

1. In this Act the phrase 'to walk a dog' is given its natural meaning and includes exercising a dog whether on or off a leash and running with a dog.

Schedule 2

Repeals

1. This Act repeals the Dog Exercise Act 1993

                              The Schedules

Figure 3.4 Features of Acts of Parliament

twenty-first Act to be passed in 2015, which is why it is Chapter 21. As it happens, the citation is very rarely used when referring to an Act of Parliament; the short title and year are usually sufficient.

- *Long title*: The long title gives a brief description of the general scope of the Act.
- *Date of Royal Assent*: Royal Assent is the final stage for a Bill to become an Act of Parliament.
- *Enacting formula*: In effect, this states that the Act has been passed by the House of Lords (the Lords Temporal and Spiritual) and the House of Commons and has received Royal Assent. Where legislation is enacted using the procedure under the Parliament Acts 1911 and 1949 – and so not passed with the consent of the House of Lords – the enacting formula is phrased differently to recognise that fact and reads:

> Be it enacted by The Queen's most Excellent Majesty, by and with the advice and consent of the Commons in this present Parliament assembled, in accordance with the provisions of the Parliament Acts 1911 and 1949, and by the authority of the same, as follows:–

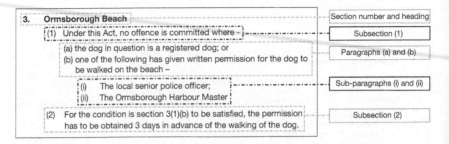

Figure 3.5 FA section with subsections, paragraphs and sub-paragraphs

- *The sections*: These are the main provisions of the Act and are divided into sections, subsections, paragraphs and sub-paragraphs. Figure 3.5 shows an additional section of my fictional Walking Dogs (Ormsborough Beach) Act 2015, with subsections, paragraphs and sub-paragraphs.
- *The schedules*: Schedules are found at the end of many Acts of Parliament and often contain additional detail; they may also state which other statutes the Act repeals or amends.

3.4.1   Understanding legislation

As with case law, there are different methods you can use to help you understand the meaning of a legislative provision:

- You can look at what your textbook says the provision in question means.
- Modern legislation is accompanied by Explanatory Notes, which give a summary of the Act and explain each of its provisions in plain English. These Explanatory Notes, and the legislation they accompany, are available on the government's website: www.legislation.gov.uk/
- There are sometimes explanatory texts that are published to explain the background and meaning of some of the more significant statutes. For example, guidance about the Human Rights Act 1998 may be found in: J. Wadham, H. Mountfield and A. Edmundson (2015) *Blackstone's Guide to the Human Rights Act 1998*, 7th edn, Oxford. UK: OUP.

3.5   TEXTBOOKS

The primary purpose of textbooks is to provide a general explanation of a particular area of law. Sometimes, textbook authors will also make some critique or commentary of the legal position, or suggest what the law should be taken to be, but their primary purpose is to explain. Most textbooks are written for a student readership, though some are directed at, and are used by, academics and practitioners.

For any one subject, there will be textbooks of varying levels of complexity. At one end of the spectrum, we have the very simple, short texts that are primarily aimed at providing an uncomplicated account of the basics of the subject. Usually, it is not intended that students use these as their sole textbook, and they are often marketed as helping students prepare for exams. These books can be very useful in helping you to understand the basics and as an aid to help you cope with the more complicated texts. It can also be useful for you to read the relevant chapter or chapters of books of this kind before a lecture. Doing so will mean that you have some prior understanding of the subject matter of the lecture before you attend it, which will mean that you are better able to understand and engage with the class.

TIP BOX

It will be useful to read the relevant chapter, or chapters, of one of the simpler, more accessible textbooks before a lecture so that you have some prior knowledge of the subject matter which will, in turn, help you better understand and engage with the class.

In the middle of the spectrum are slightly longer textbooks that are quite accessible and are directly aimed at a student undergraduate market. These can be, and are often intended to be, the main textbook that students rely on for any particular subject.

At the far end of the spectrum are the really weighty, doorstop books. These will be about 800–900 pages in length, and you may need specialist lifting equipment just to carry them around. The target audience for these texts includes students, academics and practitioners.

It is likely that, for each of your modules, the module leader will recommend a particular textbook that you should purchase, to which they will make reference throughout the module. These will often be books from the middle, more accessible part of the spectrum, the type marketed directly at students. Your lecturer will believe that such books are useful because they are written in a way to help students quickly understand.

A lecturer may, though, worry that, if they recommend a book that is too simplistic, the students may outgrow it as they develop their understanding, and it may not be sufficiently challenging for the more able students. Because of this, you may find that the leader of a particular module you are taking will recommend that you purchase a book from the weighty, doorstop end of the spectrum. This will partly be because they enjoy inflicting pain and suffering on poor students, and partly (and really) because such books represent the level of understanding that lecturers want their students to achieve.

Whatever textbook your lecturer recommends, it is a worthwhile strategy to make use of books of different levels of complexity. That is, use books at the simpler, more accessible end of the spectrum to help you understand the basics and then refer to books of the more complicated type to help you develop the depth and sophistication of your understanding.

3.5.1   Purchasing textbooks

It is common for the leader of a module to recommend a particular textbook for you to purchase for their subject. If they do, then this is the book that you should purchase if you can. This is because they will most likely ask you to read particular pages of it in preparation for class.

If, however, you are given a choice of which textbook to buy, or are buying a supplementary one, you should keep the following principles in mind:

- *Read before you buy*: You should always read a book before you purchase it to see if it is written in a way you find readable. You should spend some time in the bookshop or library reading different books to identify those whose authors' writing style you find most accessible. Most online bookstores also have a facility where you can read extracts from books before you purchase them, to allow you to choose the correct textbook for you. Remember, for books of all levels of complexity, some authors are simply better than others at conveying their meaning.
- *Beware of buying books that are too basic*: Textbooks at the more simplistic end of the spectrum may be very accessible – and, for that reason, may appear to be an appropriate purchase – but they may lack the depth to enable you to develop the sufficient level of understanding required of an undergraduate student (though, as I mention in Section 3.5 above and Section 3.5.2 below, they may be useful to help you understand some of the more complicated texts).

- *Be careful when buying second-hand books*: You may be able to save money by buying second hand books. You should, though, be aware of the date of publication and whether the book is the latest edition. Law is a subject that can change significantly very quickly, and it is usually the case that you should not purchase a book that is not the latest edition or is very out of date. Having said that, some subjects do not alter very much from year to year – at least as far as undergraduates are concerned; jurisprudence is an example.

3.5.2   Reading and making use of textbooks

As a first-year undergraduate student, one of the first subjects I studied was contract law. I purchased the book recommended by the module leader. This was a very weighty tome of more than 900 pages and is one of the leading texts in the subject, relied on by academics, practitioners and even judges. As a new and conscientious law student – and because I did not know better – I decided that I had to read and understand this book from cover to cover, and so I dutifully began reading at page 1. Within a couple of pages, I was struggling to understand, and it became absolutely apparent that I would never read all of the book.

Of course, I had adopted a ridiculously over-ambitious technique to begin with. Textbooks are not meant to be read in the same way as a novel – fully, from end to end. Rather, they are tools to help you understand the law, and you should use them as needed. Instead of attempting to read a book from start to finish, you should read only those parts that are relevant. So, if you are trying to get to grips with promissory estoppel in contract law, you should read the chapter – or the pages – that explain this concept. It is likely that your lecturer will direct you to the relevant chapter or pages that they wish you to read. If not, or if you are reading a textbook other than that recommended by your lecturer, you can simply make use of the contents page at the beginning of the book and the index at the end to find the pages where – in my example – promissory estoppel is discussed.

If you are struggling to understand the textbook you are reading, make use of one of the simpler ones to help you understand the basics and then progress to the more complicated book.

TIP BOX

Use simple, accessible textbooks to get to grips with the basics of a subject and as stepping stones to help you understand the more complicated texts.

You may also find it useful to try to write your own brief and basic account of the area of law you are trying to understand or to attempt to explain it to a friend. Attempting to paraphrase what you read will enable you to identify and understand the fundamental aspects of the topic, which you can then use to build up a more complex and nuanced appreciation of it.

TIP BOX

If you are finding it difficult to understand something you are reading, try to explain it to a friend or write your own basic account of it. This will help you understand the fundamentals and may help you to identify those particular aspects of the topic with which you are especially struggling.

If you are still finding it difficult to understand what you read, try to book some time with the relevant lecturer so that he or she can attempt to help. This should not, though, be your first port of call. You should put the work in to attempt to understand before you approach your lecturer: they will be thoroughly unimpressed if you turn up saying, in essence, 'I've done nothing and I still can't understand' (which happens more frequently than you might imagine). It is usually best to try to arrange help from your lecturer by email and to give them some brief detail of what it is you are finding difficult. Doing this will mean that they can arrange a time when they are free and can prepare to advise you.

COMMON ERROR

Do not seek help from your lecturer without first putting in the time and effort to understand. For a start, your lecturer will not be pleased if you seek their help without making a real attempt to figure things out for yourself. Secondly, they will be better able to help you if you have some base knowledge on which they can build.

Even if you are not struggling to understand what you read, it is still useful to read about the same topic in different textbooks. This will expose you to different points of view and different ways of expressing the same thing, which will help you develop a more rounded, nuanced appreciation of it.

WORK SMARTER

Reading about the same aspect of law in different textbooks will expose you to different points of view and different ways of referring to the same thing which will, consequently, help you to develop a better, more sophisticated understanding of it.

In addition, as I write in Section 6.5 of Chapter 6, if you inform your coursework – and make it clear to your marker, via your references and bibliography, that you have informed your work – with a variety of material, then your marker will probably recognise the effort you have put in, and you are likely to receive better marks.

Highlighting

You may find it useful to highlight parts of the text that you think are particularly relevant or that you think you may want to make use of when writing coursework. Of course, there are highlighter pens that are manufactured for this purpose. I do not use these but simply use a pencil line drawn vertically in the outside margin of the page to identify any text I think particularly relevant (I do this in large part because I have a somewhat pathetic reverence for books and think highlighter pens irreversibly damage them). I also make use of page markers (small plastic or paper tabs) to identify the pages I find interesting.

COMMON ERROR

Students often highlight so much text that they leave hardly anything unmarked. For fairly obvious reasons, this is pointless and defeats the purpose of highlighting which is to identify particular passages that are relevant or interesting.

3.6   JOURNAL ARTICLES AND CHAPTERS IN EDITED COLLECTIONS

You should try to read, and inform your work with, journal articles and chapters from edited texts throughout your degree. Journal articles and chapters in edited collections are written by academics, practising lawyers and judges and are usually aimed at other academics or practitioners. They attempt to do any of a number of things, including:

- critique a particular area of law or point of view;
- attempt to provide a theoretical rationale for a particular area of law;
- explain a particular area of law; or
- explain the implications of a particular case or legislative provision.

Reading journal articles and chapters from edited texts means that you will be exposed to different, and sometimes complex, arguments, which will help to develop your understanding. It will also give you some indication of the quality to which you should aspire in your own writing. Moreover, as with textbooks, reading a variety of materials and demonstrating to your markers that you have informed your work with them will mean that they are more likely to award higher marks.

Students often find journal articles and chapters from edited texts particularly difficult to understand. This is no doubt because they are usually primarily aimed at a better-informed readership (such as academics). There are, though, some techniques you can adopt to help you understand:

- Look in the bibliography of your textbook to see if the article or chapter in question is listed. If it is, look for the author's name in the index to try to find the pages where the article is mentioned. It may be that the textbook gives a brief summary of the argument made in the article.
- Similarly, if you have access to a cases and materials book, this might give an extract from, and an explanation of, the article or chapter.
- Many articles and book chapters will contain an abstract. This is usually at the front of the piece and provides a brief summary of the argument being made.
- For journal articles, even if there is no abstract at the start of the piece, there may be a basic summary of it on Westlaw, and you can use the journal article search facility to access this.
- It might aid you if you carefully read the introduction and conclusion to get a summary of the argument made. This will help because the introduction will be written so as to indicate to readers what they are about to read, and the conclusion will summarise the main points made in the piece.
- You might find it useful to try to give an account of the article or book chapter to a friend, or to write a brief overview of it. This will help you to ascertain the basics of the argument being made, which you can then build on with further reading.

- You may find if beneficial to quickly skim-read the journal article or chapter and to take note of the different subheadings. This will give you some indication of the structure of the piece, which will aid your understanding when you read it properly.

3.7   COMMON LATIN TERMS

You will come across a number of Latin terms in your reading of secondary materials and of law reports. Table 3.6 attempts to give you an indication of the meaning and use of some of the more common terms. (I give an account of some Latin terms that are often used when referencing in Table 10.1 of Chapter 10.)

Table 3.6 Latin terms and their meanings

Latin term	Meaning
a fortiori	'For this stronger reason': used to say that, if a first proposition is taken to be correct, then a second one must be taken to be even more correct. For example, 'if animals should not be mistreated, then the same must be true, a fortiori, of children'
a priori	'From the earlier': used for things that are knowable simply by an understanding of language rather than because of experience of the world. So, I know, a priori, that all Labradors are canines, but my knowledge that Labradors like having their bellies tickled is not a priori knowledge but is based on experience
actus reus	'Guilty act': the factual element of a crime. If I hit and kill someone in my car, the fact of killing them is the *actus reus*; whether I am guilty of a crime, and if so what crime, depends on my *mens rea* – my mental state; I will be guilty of murder only if I intended to kill or grievously harm the person I hit
ad hoc	'For this': refers to something created or done for a particular purpose or as and when necessary. So, if I say that I will deal with any complaints about the quality of my writing in an ad hoc manner, I mean that, rather than plan ahead and adopt a general strategy for dealing with complaints, I will deal with them as and when they arise
amicus curiae	'Friend of the court': often used to refer to a person who is not a party to a case but has a strong interest in it and is permitted to make representations

Table 3.6 continued

Latin term	Meaning
audi alteram partem	'Hear the other side': the principle that no one should have a judgment made against them without being given the opportunity to present their side of the case
bona fide	'In good faith': usually used to refer to the honest motives of the person involved – 'He made a bona fide offer to purchase the car'. It may also be used to indicate the genuineness of something, e.g. 'Despite appearances to the contrary, Dr McGarry is a bona fide legal expert'
caveat emptor	'Buyer beware': indicates that those buying goods should inspect them with regard to quality and suitability. This principle has been significantly modified in modern consumer law
circa	'Around' or 'about': 'The courts seemed to be more willing to hold the government to account from circa the 1960s.' Sometimes abbreviated as simply '*c.*'
de facto	'In fact' or 'in reality': 'Legally, the Queen is the head of government in the UK but, de facto, it is the prime minister'
de jure	'In law': 'Although the prime minister, for all intents and purposes, leads the government in the UK, *de jure*, the monarch is its head'
et al.	An abbreviation of 'et alia' meaning 'and others'. It is commonly used where a book has a number of authors and the writer wants a shortened way to refer to it. For example, 'See *Blackstone's Guide to the Human Rights Act 1998* by Wadham et al.'
ex officio	'From the office': used to refer to someone having a position on a body by virtue of the office they hold. For example: 'McGarry is an *ex officio* member of the committee'
ex parte	'From (alternatively "by" or "for") a party': often used where a case is brought on behalf of another. For example, in the past, the name of judicial review cases was formulated as: *R v Secretary of State for the Home Department, ex parte Fire Brigades Union* [1995] 2 AC 513, meaning 'The Crown (R) against the Secretary of State on behalf of the Fire Brigades Union'
habeas corpus	'You have the body': usually an action whereby a court orders that a person detaining another satisfies the court that the detention is lawful

Table 3.6 continued

Latin term	Meaning
inter alia	'Among other things': e.g. 'McGarry's book is, inter alia, an ideal birthday gift'
intra vires	'Within the powers': used when saying that a body has not exceeded its legal powers
ipso facto	'By that very fact': for instance, 'Clare's shooting of Joe was witnessed by dozens of people and so, *ipso facto*, it was obvious she was guilty'
mala fide	The opposite of bona fide, means 'in (or with) bad faith'
mens rea	'Guilty mind': the element of a crime that relies on the state of the defendant's mind. So, for instance, the *mens rea* of murder is to intend to kill or cause grievous bodily harm, and so, even if one is responsible for another's death, it is only a murder if this *mens rea* (intent) is present
mutatis mutandis	'Making the necessary changes': commonly used when stating that two things are similar if you take the differences into account, or saying that one thing can be adapted for another purpose if you make certain alterations. So, you might write: 'I treat all my employees, *mutatis mutandis*, the same', or, 'This contract may be adapted, *mutatis mutandis*, for your purposes also'
nemo judex in causa sua	'No one should be a judge in their own cause': the rule against bias, that those making a decision should have nothing to gain or lose from that decision
obiter dicta/obiter dictum	'By the way' (dictum is singular, dicta is plural): comments made by a judge that are not the reason for deciding the case and do not, therefore, compose the binding part of the judgment
per se	'In itself': one might say, 'I have nothing against EU law, per se, it's just that I have never found it to be interesting'
prima facie	'On the face of it': used to refer to how things first appear – 'Prima facie, on paper, Joseph looked like he was going to be an exemplary student'
pro bono	Abbreviation of 'pro bono publico', meaning 'for the public good': commonly used to refer to work undertaken by lawyers for free

Table 3.6 continued

Latin term	Meaning
quid pro quo	'Something for something': usually used to refer to a reciprocal arrangement whereby one party gives a thing in return for something else
ratio decidendi	'The reason for the decision': refers to the parts of a judgment that are the reasons for it being decided one way rather than another. For decisions of the senior courts, the *ratio decidendi* is the binding part of the judgment
sic	'Thus': placed in quotations, usually in square brackets, to indicate that the person using the quotation has copied it correctly and has noticed a mistake in the original. So, for instance, 'McGarry writes that "Dogs is [*sic*] better than cats"'. It is a way for the person using the quotation to say 'I've spotted the mistake but this is how it was originally written'.
ultra vires	'Beyond the powers': often used in public law and company law to state that a body has exceeded its legal powers
viz.	This is an abbreviation of videlicet and is used to mean 'namely' or 'that is'. For instance, 'I've purchased McGarry's latest attempt to fund his extravagant lifestyle, viz. *Acing the LLB*.'

Chapter 4
An introduction to assessments

This chapter will:

- introduce you to the different types and methods of assessment that you will commonly meet during your degree;
- discuss the requirements of submitting coursework and dissertations;
- mention the procedures your institution will have if you miss an assessment for an unavoidable and unexpected reason;
- discuss different forms of academic malpractice and the potential consequences for those found guilty of, and how to avoid, them;
- talk about the importance of receiving, and acting on, the feedback for the work you produce.

4.1   INTRODUCTION

The purpose of this chapter is to introduce you to the different types and methods of assessment that you are likely to encounter as an undergraduate law student. These will be considered in more detail in the following chapters.

This chapter will also discuss: submitting your work, what to do if you miss an assessment because of an unexpected and unavoidable circumstance, academic malpractice and how to avoid it, and the importance of obtaining and acting on feedback about your work.

4.2   TYPES AND METHODS OF ASSESSMENT

As an undergraduate student, you will be assessed in a variety of ways. This is to test an array of different skills – oral and written communication, problem solving, research skills, etc. – and to allow you to demonstrate the scope of your abilities. It is likely that you will be assessed in the following ways.

Exams

It is likely that you will have been assessed by examination at some point prior to your degree. As an undergraduate, you will most certainly be subjected to examinations. These may take a number of forms, including: seen or unseen (that is, whether or not you have sight of the examination before you sit it), and open or closed book (whether you will be able to take your textbook or notes into the examination).

Chapter 7 gives more details about the different types of exam that you may encounter and about how you may maximise your chances of doing well.

Coursework

As with exams, you will certainly be assessed by coursework throughout your degree. Coursework may be defined as answering a question set by the lecturer where you research and write your answer away from the classroom and submit it by a specified date.

Chapter 6 discusses coursework and how to answer it to the best of your abilities.

Dissertations

It is very likely that you will have the opportunity, and may even be obliged, to undertake a dissertation during your degree, usually in your final year. Dissertations are substantial research projects that you research and write outside the classroom, under the guidance of one of your lecturers as supervisor.

Chapter 9 gives more information about dissertations, about their advantages and disadvantages for students and about how you may successfully complete one.

Presentations, moots and assessed seminars

You will most likely be required to do presentations during your degree. These may compose part of the formal assessment of a particular module or may simply be something that is unassessed but that you are required to do.

You will also be provided with the opportunity to moot, and this might form part of the way you are assessed. A moot is a fictional appeal case where issues of law – rather than the facts of the case – are in dispute. Usually, there are two mooting teams, each with two members, who argue the case before a judge.

Assessed seminars are becoming more common in higher-education institutions. They operate in a similar manner to unassessed seminars, in that they are a learning forum that you are expected to prepare for and participate in; they differ in that you will be awarded a mark for your preparation, participation, level of understanding and, perhaps, other factors.

Chapter 8 looks at presentations, moots and assessed seminars and provides advice about how to best undertake them.

Problem and essay questions

As a law student, there are two types of question with which you will be presented more than any other: problem questions and essay questions. You will come across these in coursework and exams, and perhaps in other forms of assessment.

Briefly, problem questions pose a fictional scenario where a number of events of legal significance occur to different characters. You are usually asked to advise one or more of these characters about their legal rights, duties, obligations or liabilities. In essay questions, you are usually presented with a statement or proposition about an area of law that you are then asked to 'discuss', 'analyse' or in some other way evaluate.

Chapter 5 discusses problem and essay questions in full, and Chapters 6 and 7 look at how you can best answer them in coursework and exams.

4.2.1   Formative and summative assessment

As a student, you may come across the following terms: formative assessment and summative assessment.

Typically, with formative assessment, you will complete an assessment type – say coursework, a class test or even an exam – and receive feedback and a mark for that assessment. However, the mark will not count towards the final mark you receive for the module in question. In essence, it allows you to have a trial run at being assessed and to receive guidance on how you may improve.

This differs from summative assessment, where the mark you receive will normally form part of the overall mark you are awarded.

It is common to be asked to complete formative assessments in the first year of your degree so that you can learn what is expected of you as an undergraduate student and get some feedback before the marks start to count. Indeed, it is sometimes the case that the first year of a full-time degree – and the part-time equivalent – is seen as formative because, usually, it is not taken into account when the final degree classification is calculated.

You should take all opportunities to complete formative assessment and receive any feedback. A few years ago, one of my first-year students did not complete a formative assessment I set, on the basis that 'the mark didn't count'. Because of this, he missed his first chance to obtain feedback at higher-education level; he went on to fail the following summative assessment in the module, which he almost certainly would not have done had he completed the formative work and taken on board my feedback.

4.3   SUBMITTING YOUR WORK

For coursework and dissertations, you will be provided with a submission date and time. You will also be informed how you should submit your work. You may be required: to submit a hard (i.e. paper) copy of your work by hand; or to submit an electronic version of your work, often via a virtual learning environment; or to submit both a hard copy *and* an electronic version.

You must submit your work in the way specified. Do not assume you will be permitted to submit your work in any way you choose. For instance, do not assume that you can simply email your work to your lecturer in the belief that, if they have a copy of it, you have submitted. If you do not submit in the manner stipulated, you may find that your lecturer simply ignores (in my example) your email, and you are recorded as having not submitted, which may result in a mark of zero.

If you are not sure how you are expected to submit your coursework, find out from one of your lecturers or other official source. Moreover, if there is something about the process that you do not know – for instance, where the submission box is, or how to submit online – make certain you find out well in advance of submitting.

As for the submission deadline, do not assume that this is flexible. If you are required to hand in coursework by 4 p.m. on a specified date, do not assume that you will be fine if you are a few minutes late. It is not unheard of for students to be recorded as having submitted their work late – and to have their mark reduced as a consequence – even though they were merely a couple of minutes past the deadline.

4.3.1   Missing an assessment owing to an unavoidable circumstance

All institutions will have procedures to deal with situations where students miss an assessment because of some unexpected, unavoidable circumstance – for instance, if a student is ill on the day of an exam.

It will often be the case that short extensions to coursework submission dates may be granted by one of your lecturers in the law school. Other situations may require approval to be given by some institutional body or committee that is external to the law school. In all cases, you are probably required to provide evidence to substantiate the reason why you missed the assessment or why you need an extension.

Moreover, where possible, you should obtain authorisation for the extension to the submission date or missed assessment beforehand. Of course, this will not always be possible, and your institution's procedures and principles will recognise this; however, if you could have sought prior authorisation for, say, an extension, but failed to do so, you may be penalised.

Extensions and the like will normally be given where, for instance, sudden illness or a significant bereavement means that it is appropriate. You should, though, bear in mind that there will be some circumstances for which you will not be granted an extension or permitted to retake an assessment at a later date without penalty. So, it is often the case that extensions will not be given for:

- poor time management (e.g. you did not leave yourself enough time to complete a piece of coursework);
- employment problems;
- travel problems;
- computer or printer failure (with the former, you are expected to take reasonable steps to save your work and make back-up copies).

TIP BOX

A quick and easy way to make a back-up copy of the latest version of your work is to email it to yourself.

4.4   PLAGIARISM AND OTHER MALPRACTICE

As a law student, you will have no doubt earned the admiration of your family and friends. In fact, when you announced that you had a place on a law degree, some in your social or family circle may have looked at you as if you had just announced that you were to become a brain surgeon or that NASA had just commissioned you to design their next rocket. The pride of your relations and acquaintances is no doubt well earned. Imagine, then, how it would feel to have to tell all those who had previously delighted in your success that you were being expelled from your degree because you had been caught cheating.

I hope none of my readers ever contemplates any kind of academic malpractice. Unfortunately, I know from experience that this is unlikely; I know that, every week, in higher-education institutions across the land, disciplinary action is being taken against students for some form of cheating, and that the likelihood is that this will happen to some who read this.

When it is discovered, academic malpractice is extremely unpleasant for all those involved. Lecturers find themselves having to spend time and effort gathering evidence against one of their students. The accused student finds themself in a rather scary atmosphere, where all their career plans may be under threat and where they may have to tell their friends and family some unpleasant facts.

There are different forms of academic malpractice and they all involve some attempt to gain advantage by unfair or inappropriate means. Some of the most common include the following:

- *Cheating in exams*: There are various ways in which students may attempt to cheat in exams, including:
  - taking into the examination venue, and consulting, written material that is not permitted;
  - attempting to communicate with others in the exam;
  - having someone sit the examination in their place (impersonation).
- *Collusion or copying*: Collusion occurs where two or more students work together and produce work that is meant to be the unaided work of one or both of them. Copying occurs where one or more students access and rely on the work of another without their consent.
- *Plagiarism*: Plagiarism is where one person attempts to pass off another's work or ideas as their own. It may occur where work is copied verbatim – word for word – or where the work submitted is changed from the original but in substance remains the same and, crucially, is unacknowledged.

COMMON ERROR

It is not sufficient to avoid a charge of plagiarism to simply change the words from the source material. If you take someone else's work and attempt to pass it off as your own – i.e.: without acknowledgement – simply by paraphrasing (by changing some or all of the words but leaving the substance) then it is plagiarism.

4.4.1 Consequences of malpractice

The consequences of being found guilty of academic malpractice can be literally life changing. For the severest cases, the student may be withdrawn from their degree and their institution. In fact, even after graduation, if it is later discovered that a student cheated in order to obtain their degree, the degree can be retrospectively withdrawn.

Even where a student is not thrown off their course after a finding of malpractice, the consequences may still be significant for their future careers. In the first place, those who wish to work as practising lawyers may be asked to provide the names of academic referees (i.e. their lecturers). Because of the importance placed on the personal integrity of those working in the legal profession, it is often the case that referees are specifically asked to declare whether or not the student has ever been found to have committed any form of academic malpractice. Moreover, as an applicant wishing to join the profession, you may be asked to declare any finding of malpractice against you. A statement by either your referees or yourself that you have been found guilty of academic malpractice may cause you some difficulties in your path to becoming a practising lawyer and, in serious cases, may disbar you altogether.

Even where your lecturer is not specifically asked to make a declaration about academic malpractice, most reference requests – for legal and non-legal employment – particularly ask the referee to comment on the applicant's honesty. If you have been found guilty of cheating in one of your assessments, your lecturer will be obliged to mention that in the reference they provide.

In brief, the risks and possible consequences of engaging in academic malpractice outweigh the potential benefits.

4.4.2 The ease of spotting malpractice

I have long thought that, if students knew how easy it is for markers to detect plagiarism and other forms of cheating, they would not even be tempted to try it. This is probably wishful thinking on my part, but it is a fact that academic malpractice is very easy to detect.

With regard to cheating in examinations, invigilators and institutions have various means – of differing levels of sophistication – of detecting cheating. For instance, it is not uncommon for an invigilator to appear to be reading while covertly watching a student who is acting suspiciously (and this, in itself, is easy to spot in a room full of students who are mostly working away).

With collusion or copying, your marker will quickly notice if you use a phrase that has been used in one of the other pieces that they are marking and that is not a quotation. Markers also spot copying and collusion because of similarities in the structure of students' work.

Plagiarism is also more easily detected than you might imagine. For a start, it is increasingly common for students to be required to submit electronic versions of their work via plagiarism detection software.

Apart from this, lecturers will simply be able to spot plagiarised work because of their experience. One of the commonest ways is based on of the quality of the work – as a marker, if you begin to read work that is grammatically correct and phrased in a way that you would not necessarily find in the work of an undergraduate student who is relatively new to the subject, then you become suspicious. This is all the more the case if the student's work varies in quality so that, in some parts, it is perfectly written, whereas, in others, the writing is decidedly ropey (the student may not be aware of the differing quality of their work, but an experienced lecturer certainly will be).

Furthermore, your lecturer is likely to be very familiar with the work that you may be tempted to pass off as your own. In the first place, you are unlikely to be the first student to rely on that information, and so your lecturer may have seen it in student work many times before. Second, your lecturer may simply be familiar with the work because they have come across it as a teacher or researcher; for example, one of my colleagues once spotted an instance of plagiarism because the passage in question was taken from an article that he (my colleague) had reviewed as part of the editorial process prior to the article being published.

It is worth remembering here that your work may be read by up to three different people: the first marker of your work, the second marker and the external examiner. This obviously increases the chance of any plagiarised material being spotted.

I end this subsection with a personal anecdote. A few years ago, my wife (who is also an academic) and I went to buy a car. While the salesman was accompanying us on the test drive, he asked us what we did for a living. On hearing that we are lecturers, he told us that he'd been thrown off his degree course for plagiarism. He said that he was surprised that he'd been caught, because the material he'd copied had been taken from the Internet, from page 27 of the results returned by his search engine. However, although he may have thought he'd found an obscure source to copy – because it was on page 27 of the results pages – what he didn't seem to appreciate was that, once his marker had entered the suspect text into a search engine, it would return the source as result 1 on page 1. We both decided not to tell him this as our desire to be smart alecs was outweighed by our desire to get a good deal on the car. We did, though, have some concerns about the honesty of our seller.

4.4.3   Avoiding malpractice

Advising you how to avoid some kinds of malpractice is easy, because it simply involves me writing:

- Don't cheat in exams!
- Don't collude with anyone else to produce work that is meant to be your own unaided effort!
- Don't copy someone else's work!

However, I guess my contractual obligations with the good folks at my publishers require me to write a little more. And, in fact, as far is plagiarism is concerned, a little more is needed.

Although it is clear that some students engage in plagiarism deliberately, it is also clear that some students do not fully understand that their activities amount to plagiarism. This is particularly the case where a student takes a passage from a book, article or other source and changes the words. Indeed, some may have been told in the past that this is perfectly acceptable. Unfortunately, it is not, and it still amounts to plagiarism. Remember, plagiarism includes passing off someone else's idea as your own, even if you change the way the idea is expressed.

To avoid committing plagiarism, you simply need to adhere to the following principles:

- If you copy text verbatim, you need to enclose the text in quotation marks and provide an appropriate reference.
- Do not simply change the words of your source material. If you want to convey someone else's idea, but do not want to quote them directly (and this might be perfectly appropriate, so that your work is not merely made up of quotations), then you should write it in your own words. If you cannot do this, then it is probably the case that you do not fully understand what you are trying to convey and you should, therefore, undertake more reading.
- Whenever you are writing about someone else's ideas, even if writing in your own words, you should always provide a reference (and you should see Chapter 10 for advice about referencing).

That is not to say, however, that you must provide a reference for all that you write. As you will read in Chapter 6, Section 6.5, it is appropriate and right for you to include your own informed ideas and arguments in your work; indeed, doing so is the hallmark of a good student. When you do include your own ideas and arguments, you obviously cannot, and should not try to, provide a reference. (I make this point explicit because I have had very capable students believing that they cannot write something if they cannot provide a reference for it, which obviously stymies their ability to produce work that would achieve the top marks.)

4.5 OBTAINING FEEDBACK

Often, students repeat the same mistakes in coursework after coursework and exam after exam. Sometimes, the mistake is easily corrected, but the student is unaware of it because they have not sought, or do not read, feedback on their assessments. This is foolish, because, especially with coursework, your markers will write feedback in such a way as to advise you how to improve your performance in future work. They will identify what is good in your work but also what you could improve.

It is understandable that, when students receive their marked work back, they focus on the mark they receive. However, apart from your very last assessment, the mark is not necessarily the most important information you receive from your marker, because the comments and feedback – if you take notice of them – will help you improve in future assessments.

Given this, it is a good idea for you to take note of the feedback you receive and, if necessary and possible, book time with the marker of your work to receive feedback in person.

It is also a good idea systematically to record the main points that the feedback you receive suggests you need to improve. Table 4.1 is an example of how you might do this. Recording all your feedback in this systematic way will allow you easily to see the things that you should concentrate your efforts on improving.

Table 4.1 Recording main points of feedback across coursework

Module	Main points for improving
Public law	Spelling, grammar, referencing, read more
Torts	Spelling, referencing, more reading
Criminal law	Spelling, referencing, more reading

Chapter 5

Understanding essay questions and problem questions

This chapter will introduce you to:

- the basic structure of essay and problem questions;
- the meaning of key words commonly used in essay and problem questions;
- strategies for reading, unpacking and understanding the different parts of such questions and for recognising what it is you are being asked.

5.1   INTRODUCTION

Throughout your time as an undergraduate law student, there are two types of question that you will meet more than any other: essay questions and problem questions. You may come across these in coursework, examinations or, indeed, in any of the assessments to which you are subjected.

Generally speaking, essay questions consist of a statement about law that the students are asked to 'discuss', 'evaluate' or in some other way analyse. Problem questions pose a fictional scenario, and students are asked to advise one or more of the parties about their rights, obligations or liabilities. It is possible to have questions that do not fit neatly into these two categories or that are a combination of both. However, the advice contained in this chapter, and in Chapters 6 and 7, will be useful for all such questions.

As I make clear in the following chapters, one of the common errors made by all students is that they fail to answer the question that has been asked. This chapter attempts to help you avoid that error by enabling you fully to understand both essay and problem questions.

5.2   UNDERSTANDING ESSAY QUESTIONS

As mentioned in the introduction to this chapter, a common error made by students is to fail to answer the question asked. If you are going to avoid making this error, you need to be sure what you are being asked. To help you do this, let's examine five essay questions: a tort law essay question, two public law essay questions, a jurisprudence essay question and a contract law essay question.

1   The 'but for' test provides an easy way for the courts to determine causation in negligence, but it has often proved inadequate and may lead to injustice in complex cases.
     Critically analyse this statement.
2   Constitutional conventions are sometimes described as binding rules of constitutional behaviour. They do not, though, always operate as such in practice.
     Evaluate this statement.
3   Any fair-minded observer would agree that feminism was necessary in the nineteenth century, and even in the 1960s and 1970s. But all the battles have now been won, and feminism is no longer necessary.
     Critically discuss with reference to feminist jurisprudence.
4   Discuss whether a valid contract always requires consideration.
5   Explain how the courts have interpreted the phrase 'public authority' as used in the Human Rights Act 1998.

The format of the first three questions is fairly typical of essay questions: there is a statement, proposition or assertion about a particular aspect of law, followed by an instruction that the statement must be critically analysed, evaluated, critically discussed or examined in some other way. Such statements may be written by the lecturer, or they may be quotations from, say, academics or judges.

The format of the fourth question is different, but, in effect, the same components are present: there is an implicit assertion about the law – that valid contracts always require consideration – and an instruction, in this case to discuss the statement.

The fifth question is a little different again. There is still an instruction, in this instance to 'explain'. However, there is no assertion or proposition – the instruction is simply to explain (in this example) the way in which the courts have interpreted a particular legislative provision.

We will look at unpacking the statement part of such questions below. First, it is worth considering the instructing words typically used.

5.2.1   The instruction

There are various instructions used in questions of this sort, including those shown in Table 5.1. These words are obviously different, but they are similar and are often, in essence, asking students to do virtually the same thing: to consider – in a scholarly, balanced and academic way – the truth or correctness of the statement given.

Table 5.1 Instructions used in questions

Discuss	Evaluate	Analyse	Describe	Explain	Compare and contrast

Let's look at the meaning of these different instructing words. At first glance, the words seem to divide into two basic types:

- words that are asking for a mere description or explanation ('describe', 'explain' etc.); and
- words that are asking for more depth of analysis ('discuss', 'evaluate', 'analyse', 'compare and contrast').

However, even where the instruction falls into the more descriptive category, students should still include some critical analysis in order to gain the higher marks.

So, to use the fourth question above as an example, students should do more than simply explain the way in which the courts have interpreted the words 'public authority' (though they *must* make sure they do this). To get the higher marks, they should also provide a critical analysis of the courts' decisions in this area, drawing on judicial comments (including from minority judgments), the work of academics and their own informed opinion (see Chapter 6, Section 6.5, for more advice on how to do this).

The instructions that you will commonly meet as a student may be interpreted as shown in Table 5.2.

Table 5.2 Instructions and their interpretations

Discuss	You are expected to consider conflicting arguments with regard to the statement in the question. So, in Question 4 above, you are expected to consider arguments that consideration is always a necessary requirement of a valid contract against arguments that, at least at times, it is not necessary
Evaluate	This means that you should make an assessment of the validity of the statement given. So, in Question 2 above, you are being asked to consider the merit of the assertion that constitutional conventions always operate as binding rules. You would do this by considering the assertion itself against any contrasting arguments
Analyse	Here, again, you are being asked to examine the validity of the statement given. For example, in Question 1 above, students are being asked to consider – in a balanced, informed way – whether the 'but for' test provides an easy way for the courts to determine causation in negligence cases, whether it has proved inadequate, and whether it leads to possible injustice
Describe	If you are asked to 'describe', you are being asked to give an account of something. For instance, a question that asks you to 'Describe the development of the neighbour principle since *Donoghue v Stevenson*' is asking you to give an account – a description – of the development of that principle. However, bear in mind that a simple description is not sufficient to secure the higher marks: a good essay should also include some critical analysis of the way in which the principle has been developed by the courts
Explain	'Explain' is similar to 'describe' in that students are being asked to give an account. However, the word implies that more than a simple description is required. To use Question 5, above, as an example, students are not being asked simply to describe how the courts have interpreted the phrase 'public authority'; they are being asked to give an account of the courts' underlying rationales for their interpretations
Compare and contrast	Here, you are being asked to consider the similarities and differences between two or more things
Critically	Often, a question will not ask students simply to 'discuss' or 'analyse'; rather, it will ask them to 'critically discuss' or 'critically analyse'. The word 'critically', here, does not mean criticise in the sense of finding fault with. Rather, students are being asked to make an objective judgment of all sides of an argument. The instruction to be critical is often included to comply with the requirement that second- and third-year students (or their part-time equivalents) produce a more critical analysis than first-year students. However, my advice is that, regardless of their year, students should always aim to provide some critical analysis to get the higher marks

In summary, your answer must do what the instruction in the question asks of you: if the question asks you to 'explain' or 'discuss', you must ensure that you do this. However, your answer should also be scholarly, balanced and critical.

5.2.2 The statement

The next thing to consider is what it is you are being asked to discuss, analyse or critically evaluate.

It may seem like a statement of the obvious, but, in order to provide an answer that is relevant and does address the question (which you *must* do), you need to know what it is you are being asked. The following advice is given with coursework questions in mind; it can be easily adapted, however, to exam questions:

You should begin, unsurprisingly, by reading the question – a few times. Indeed, you should familiarise yourself with the question as early as possible.

My advice, though, is that, with coursework questions, you should not begin to work out what the question is asking in any serious way until you have covered the subject matter of the question in class. The reason for this is that you are unlikely to have the basic understanding necessary to prevent you going down a wrong route (which you may find hard to discount later). Moreover, when the subject matter of the question is covered in class, the lecturer may make specific reference to the question or explain something that gives you a new perspective on it.

Once the subject matter of the question has been covered in class, you should begin to deconstruct the question: to work out what is being asked. You should do this over a period of time and while engaging in some initial reading of your lecture notes and textbooks. An obvious starting point is to identify the particular subject matter of the question; this should be quite easy.

For instance, let's look again at one of our example questions from above, Question 1:

> The 'but for' test provides an easy way for the courts to determine causation in negligence but it has often proved inadequate and may lead to injustice in complex cases.
>
> Critically analyse this statement.

The question obviously concerns the 'but for' test as a test of causation in negligence cases.

Note! The question is *not* asking students to describe at length the law of negligence or tort law in general – it is specifically asking about the 'but for' test as a test of causation.

Next, you should ask yourself whether the question contains any sub-questions. For instance, in this example, there are at least three assertions that may be critically analysed:

- that the 'but for' test provides an easy way for the courts to determine causation in negligence cases;
- that the 'but for' test has often proved to be inadequate in complex cases; and
- that the 'but for' test may lead to possible injustice in complex cases.

Your answer should, therefore, seek to address – to critically analyse, as instructed – these three propositions.

There are also at least three sub-questions in Question 3 above:

> Any fair-minded observer would agree that feminism was necessary in the nineteenth century, and even in the 1960s and 1970s. But all the battles have now been won, and feminism is no longer necessary.
>
> Critically discuss with reference to feminist jurisprudence.

The three sub-questions are:

- whether a fair-minded observer would agree that feminism was necessary in the nineteenth century;
- whether a fair-minded observer would agree that feminism was necessary in the 1960s and 1970s; and
- whether all the battles have been won, and feminism is no longer necessary.

Again, when answering a question like this, you should address all three parts of the question. It is obvious, though, that the third sub-question – that all the battles have been won, and feminism is no longer necessary – is the most controversial part of the question and should, for that reason, form (by far) the main part of any answer.

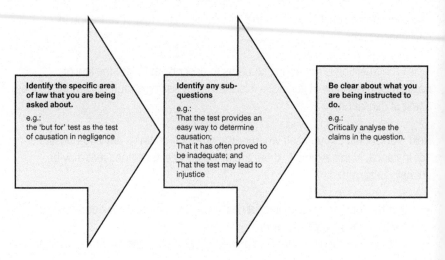

Figure 5.1 Steps to work out what an essay question is asking

When unpacking questions, you need to be careful not to read into the question assertions that are not there (but that you might wish were). For instance, in the past, I have set students questions on constitutional conventions similar to Question 2 above. Over the years, I have had many students attempting to answer a sub-question (which has not been present) about whether the UK has a constitution. This part of their answer is irrelevant, and it not only fails to earn them any marks, it also creates the overall impression that they do not fully understand and cannot distinguish the relevant from the irrelevant.

So, in brief, when working out what an essay question is asking, you should take the steps shown in Figure 5.1.

5.3   UNDERSTANDING PROBLEM QUESTIONS

Problem questions are used extensively to assess law students, usually in coursework and examinations. Problem questions commonly consist of a fictional scenario where a number of (frequently unlikely) events befall various characters; you will often be asked to provide legal advice to, or comment on the legal liability of, one or more of the parties in the scenario. As above, the following advice is particularly relevant for answering coursework questions but can be easily adapted for examinations.

Table 5.3 presents an example of a typical problem question.

Table 5.3 Example problem question

> Leo Sprog is the MP for Ormsborough West. He is in the process of introducing a private members' Bill in Parliament that would authorise the building of new houses on land in Ormsborough that was previously designated as green belt land. The passing of the Bill would enable Shark Developments, who own the land, to build a new housing estate. The Bill is opposed in Parliament by the MP for Ormsborough East, Arthur Brick.
>
> Barry Shark, managing director of Shark Developments, states, in the course of a telephone conversation with Leo Sprog: 'Our main opponent in this matter is a hypocrite and a philanderer. He didn't object when houses were built by Dodgy Housing plc, but then he has shares in that company'.
>
> During a debate on the Bill in the House of Commons, Leo Sprog ignores the rules on parliamentary language and accuses Arthur Brick of being a hypocrite. He repeats this accusation in a letter to the local paper, *The Ormsborough Star*, which has recently written a number of articles critical of Mr Brick.
>
> Arthur Brick is happily married, though he had an affair with his secretary 15 years previously. He has never owned any shares in Dodgy Housing plc.
>
> Advise Arthur Brick of any legal claims he may have.

This is quite a basic example of a problem question, and yet it contains the elements often found in such questions: it is a fictional scenario made up of a number of events and characters, and you are asked to advise one of the parties whether he has any legal claims.

Problem questions often end with an instruction or a question, for example:

- Advise Arthur Brick of any legal claims he may have.
- Advise Kevin of his liability in negligence.
- What contractual claims does Martin have?
- Describe any criminal offences that have been committed.

This instruction or question is the rubric and is, in essence, the question that you must answer.

Let's look at some initial advice with regard to problem questions.

5.3.1 Read the question

You should read the question several times to make sure that you are fully acquainted with all its aspects. You may find it useful to read the question out loud (only do this with a coursework question: reading aloud in examinations will not endear you to your fellow students or the invigilators).

TIP BOX

Reading problem questions aloud will make you feel silly but it will also help you become completely familiar with all aspects of the question, which will help you identify any sub-issues when reading your lecture notes and textbook.

5.3.2 An initial working assumption

The fact that problem questions are fictional allows you to make an initial working assumption (which you may modify): that all the information you are given is important and relevant, and that you are being given this information so that you may comment on its legal implications.

Let me illustrate my point here by asking you to imagine you are working as a solicitor in a local practice. One day, a client comes to see you because they believe a local builder they have contracted to do some work on their property has not completed the work to a sufficient standard. During the course of your interview with them to elicit the facts, they tell you that:

- they are particularly 'stressed' that day because one of their children has been unwell in school;
- they decided to undertake the building work after a family holiday in Spain;
- the builder was recommended by a friend; and
- their car is due for a service.

Part of your job, as their solicitor, will be to filter out all the legally irrelevant facts from the legally relevant, so that you can provide them with the appropriate advice.

The same is not true with problem questions. This is because all the information in the question has been deliberately provided by its writer, who knows the area of law with which the question deals. This is why you may begin with the assumption that all the information in the question is given for a reason.

So, in the above question, which (as I'm sure many of you will have guessed) concerns defamation:

- it is relevant that some assertions made about Arthur Brick were in writing and some were spoken, because this allows you to identify the spoken words as slander and the written words as libel and to advise accordingly;
- it is relevant that, during the course of the telephone conversation between Barry Shark and Leo Sprog, Mr Shark does not name Mr Brick, because this allows you to discuss the issue of whether it may be inferred that Mr Shark's remarks can only be taken to refer to Mr Brick;
- it is relevant that Leo Sprog makes the same accusation in the House of Commons and in a letter to the local paper, because, in defamation, different rules apply to statements made in Parliament to those that apply to other statements;
- it is relevant that one of the accusations against Arthur Brick (that he is a philanderer) may be true (because he had had an affair with his secretary), as this allows you to make the point that one cannot be sued in defamation for statements that are true; it is also relevant that Mr Brick's affair was 15 years in the past, as this may allow you to (briefly) discuss whether it is still true to claim that he is a philanderer; and
- it is relevant that the potential defamatory claims about Mr Brick have been made to third parties (i.e. to people other than Mr Brick), because this satisfies the requirement that a defamatory statement has to be published in order to lead to liability, which means it has to be communicated to people other than the person defamed.

Moreover, given that the facts of problem questions are carefully chosen, you should ask yourself why you are being told particular facts. For instance:

- If you are being told someone's age, or details about their mental or physical health, ask yourself whether this is relevant.
- If money is mentioned, is this in itself, or the particular amount referred to, legally significant?

Of course, it may be the case that some of the information in a particular problem question is not relevant; it may be a red herring; it may also be there to allow other parts of the question to work (the fact that two of the characters in the above question are MPs is there to allow a statement to be made in Parliament, and the mention about parliamentary language simply acknowledges that the accusation made by Mr Sprog in the Commons would lead to a rebuke by the Speaker) or for some other reason (I sometimes include material in my questions to make a joke at my colleagues' expense).

Even with these qualifications in mind, it is still a good idea to adopt, as an initial working assumption (which you may modify), that all you are being told in the question is relevant, so that you should address it in your answer.

5.3.3 What advice?

As already mentioned, problem questions often ask you to 'advise' a particular party or do something similar. It is important to remember that the advice you give here is likely to be different to the advice you might give in real life.

So, in real life, you might advise a client that they may have a claim in defamation but that it is not worth the stress, time and expense it would take to pursue it. You might even be tempted to try to give moral advice and, for instance, in an answer to a family law problem question, suggest that the main protagonist should end his affair and return to his family.

You should not be tempted to do these things when answering problem questions. You are being asked to advise one or more of the characters in the problem question about their legal position and you should ensure that you do this.

I should also say that you have to do more than simply provide the minimal advice that the rubric of the question seems to allow. So, for instance, with regard to the above problem question, the rubric instructs you: 'Advise Arthur Brick of any legal claims he may have'. You could, of course, obey this instruction by writing nothing more than: 'I advise Arthur Brick that he has two potential claims in defamation: one against Bill Shark and one against Leo Sprog'. Such an answer appears to comply with the direction in the rubric, and it would be correct as far as it goes. It is, though, very far from sufficient and would get you an extremely derisory mark, if it received a mark at all.

In answers to problem questions, you must fully demonstrate to your marker the legal reasoning you have employed, and the authorities you have relied on, to arrive at your conclusions. In short, like in answers to mathematics questions, it is not enough to give the bare answer; you must also show your working out (i.e. how you have arrived at the answer).

In doing this, you must also deal with those matters that do not give rise to legal liability and that have been included in the question for you to demonstrate your understanding. For instance, in the answer to the question above, you would not simply advise Mr Brick of the claims that he has, you would also deal with the claims that he does not have but that the question suggests are a possibility: e.g. you would be expected to explain why he does not have a claim against Leo Sprog for the comments made in the House of Commons.

5.3.4 Unpacking the question and identifying the issues

Apologies for stating the obvious, but, before beginning to answer any problem question, you need to identify the issues to which it gives rise. Often, the issues and their significance will be obvious. However, if you are struggling to recognise them, you may find it useful to adopt the following systematic approach, or something similar (as ever, for exams, you have to adapt the following approach accordingly because of the constraints of time).

You may begin by listing all the characters and organisations in the question, noting their various acts or omissions and using this to help you identify the legal significance of their conduct and the potential liabilities or claims that they may have.

Deconstructing the question in this way will help you ensure that you are fully aware of all its aspects and identify all the issues to which it gives rise.

Start by listing all the characters and organisations. Table 5.4 shows all those from the example question in Section 5.3.

Next, list the actions or omissions that each of them has done and, alongside each of these, identify, if you can, whether their behaviour is likely to be neutral in terms of legal effect or, if it has legal significance, what that significance is. Also, if it seems as though the conduct would give rise to a legal liability, make a note of

Table 5.4 Characters and organisations from sample question

Leo Sprog	Parliament	Shark Developments Ltd
Barry Shark	*The Ormsborough Star*	Arthur Brick

who would be the potential claimant (or victim in criminal cases), and who would be the potential defendant.

Identifying the legal significance of the actions in the question in Section 5.3 would look like Table 5.5.

It's probably worth noting here that you need to have a broad general understanding to get you this far, so that you can identify which acts or omissions are likely to give rise to any liability, and who the potential claimants or defendants are.

The best way to have gained this broad understanding will be to have attended all lectures and seminars. This is because such attendance will provide you with a good working knowledge, thereby allowing you to begin to identify the issues.

Table 5.5 Actions and their legal significance

Action or omission	Neutral, claimant and defendant
Leo Sprog introduces a Bill into Parliament	Probably neutral (i.e. this gives rise to no legal liability) – Mr Sprog, as an MP, is perfectly entitled to do this
Arthur Brick opposes the Bill	Probably neutral
Brry Shark makes a statement to Leo Sprog over the telephone	Defamatory statement; Barry Shark – potential defendant; Arthur Brick – potential claimant
Leo Sprog makes a statement in the House of Commons	Defamatory statement; may be protected by privilege; Leo Sprog – potential defendant; Arthur Brick – potential claimant
Leo Sprog writes a letter to *The Ormsborough Star*	Defamatory statement; Leo Sprog – potential defendant; Arthur Brick – potential claimant
The Ormsborough Star has recently been critical of Arthur Brick	Neutral (on the facts given, there is nothing to suggest that the paper has acted unlawfully)

WORK SMARTER

Attending all lectures and seminars will mean that you are better able to spot the issues which arise in any particular problem question.

Attendance at all classes may also be important because your lecturer may make direct reference to the question, or to a particular aspect of it, in the class, and you will miss this if you do not attend.

If you have missed classes, or you are struggling to identify the significance of the different acts and omissions, then you need to read through the lecture notes that appear to be relevant for the question to acquaint, or reacquaint, yourself with that area of law.

It is also worth noting that some acts or omissions may have legal significance, but that they may not, in themselves, give rise to any liability. So, in a contract law problem question, part of the question may be devoted to establishing whether a contract has been formed (e.g. whether there is an offer, acceptance, consideration and an intention to enter into legal relations), but the part of the question that is concerned with whether, say, an offer has been made will not give rise to liability in itself until there is a possible breach of the contract, though it will have legal significance. For example, imagine a contract law problem question begins as shown in Figure 5.2.

There are two parties mentioned in the question so far – Kinsella's and Clare – and they have performed the actions shown in Table 5.6, with their following significance.

Kinsella's, a local store, places the following notice in its shop window on Monday morning:

> Free glamour make-over for the first 100 customers purchasing a Windy 2000 SuperStyle Hair Dryer.

Clare sees the notice and immediately goes to the nearest ATM (cash machine) to draw out the money to purchase the dryer.

Figure 5.2 Information for contract law problem question

Table 5.6 Actions and their legal significance

Action or omission	Legal significance, claimant and defendant
Kinsella's places the notice in its window	Offer or invitation to treat
Clare goes to cash machine to obtain money	Probably neutral

That is, the notice has legal significance in that it is either an offer or an invitation to treat, but it does not in itself give rise to legal liability. However, questions such as these almost invariably end with a possible breach of contract, and it will be necessary to establish whether the notice amounted to an offer when considering whether there has been a breach. That is, although the notice may not give rise to legal liability in itself, it will form part of a claim that legal liability has been incurred by one of the parties.

As well as noting the conduct of the various characters, and the legal implication of their conduct, you should also make a record of any other contextual facts given – e.g. ages, dates, intoxication, environment – and, where possible, the significance of these facts. For example, Table 5.7 shows what we could record with regard to the question in Section 5.3.

Table 5.7 Facts of the question and their significance

Fact	Significance
Leo Sprog and Arthur Brick are both MPs	This probably has no legal significance; it merely provides the context for one of the parties to make a statement about another in the House of Commons
Shark Developments Ltd owns the land on which the houses are to be built	This probably has no legal significance; it simply provides some background context for the question
Arthur Brick is happily married but had an affair 15 years ago	This has significance for whether there would be a defence of truth (formerly justification) against a claim that it was defamatory to call Mr Brick a 'philanderer'

The significant acts, omissions and other contextual facts that you have identified will be the issues on which you are expected to provide legal advice. It should also be apparent at this stage which area or areas of law the question is concerned with. Often, a question will be focused on one overarching area of law that you have studied; so, in the example question in Section 5.3, the overarching theme of the question is defamation, and all the particular issues that follow are aspects of the law of defamation.

However, sometimes question writers may mix themes, so that, for example, a tort law problem question may contain issues of, say, negligence, statutory liability, nuisance and defamation.

Once you have identified the issues with which the question deals, you should begin to read the relevant parts of your lecture and seminar notes to begin to ascertain what the law requires with regard to each of them. While doing this, you should take note of anything that is relevant and why you think it is relevant (it is

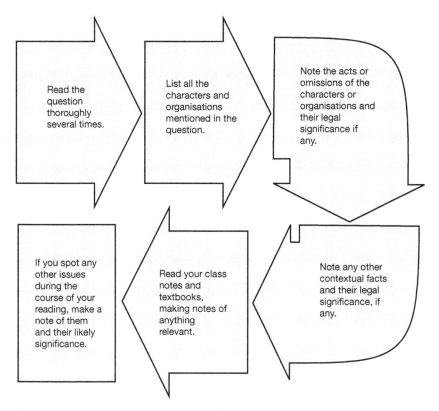

Figure 5.3 Unpacking the question and identifying the issues

important to note why a particular thing may be relevant at the moment you think of it, because you may forget later on, when you need to use it).

You should then undertake a similar exercise with the relevant parts of your textbooks, making a note of anything you feel is relevant, why it may be relevant and (importantly) where you have read it.

During the course of your reading, you may recognise some further issues inherent in the question that you did not spot in your earlier analysis. If so, record these, their likely significance and, if applicable, who the probable claimant or defendant is.

Unpacking the question in the systematic way outlined above will help you to fully understand it and to understand what the law requires with regard to each of its parts.

5.3.5 Where the law is not clear

It is almost inevitable that it will not be clear what the law requires with regard to at least part of the problem question. This will be intentional: the question writer will want to test your ability to construct a convincing argument on what the law is likely to be and, in this way, separate the better students from the less good.

Where a question does contain a 'grey' area, it is likely that your lecturer will have made reference to it in class.

As a student writing an answer to such a question, you need to identify that the law is unclear and then argue that it would probably be found to be X or Y. In making this argument, you can draw on persuasive authority including: *obiter dicta*, minority judgments, judgments from other jurisdictions and academic opinion.

TIP BOX

Where the law is unclear, do not be afraid of being bold and of making a convincing argument, supported by the most persuasive authorities you have, that the law should be taken to be one thing rather than another.

5.3.6   **Accept the facts**

It may be that the question, or a part of it, seems extremely far-fetched. You should not, though, query the facts of the question; they have been chosen by the question writer to test you on particular aspects of the law, not for their plausibility. Given this, you should accept and address the facts as given and not be tempted to argue that such things would probably not happen.

Likewise, you should not be worried about whether the facts, as presented in the question, could be proved: you might think that it would be difficult to prove that X had long harboured a grudge against Y, but, if the question states that this is the case, then, as far as you are concerned, it does not need to be proved. In the above defamation question, you might wonder whether, in real life, Mr Brick would ever become aware of the telephone conversation between Leo Sprog and Mr Shark. However, this is not real life; you have been told of the conversation so that you can comment on its legal significance.

Further, do not be tempted to introduce your own facts or suppositions to make the question more like one that you would prefer to answer.

5.3.7   **Ambiguities in the question**

It is sometimes the case that a question is ambiguous on a particular point; that is, it is not clear whether, on the information given, one thing happened or not. Such ambiguity may be deliberate on the part of the question writer, because he or she may want students to consider what the law requires for each of the alternative positions.

So, in the example problem question in Section 5.3, it is not clear whether Mr Shark has explicitly named Arthur Brick during the course of the telephone conversation, even if he does not do so in the excerpt given in the question. This allows you to make the point that, if Mr Brick is explicitly named, there is likely to be a claim in defamation, whereas, if he has not been expressly named, Mr Brick must rely on the rules of inference in order to make any claim against Mr Shark.

Similarly, it is not clear whether the newspaper publishes the letter sent to it by Mr Sprog. Speculating on this again allows you to consider the legal position if the letter is published (that the *Ormsborough Star* may also be liable in defamation) against the position if it decides not to publish.

There are two things to bear in mind here. First, make it clear to your marker what assumptions you are making with regard to any ambiguities; for instance, in answer to the above question, you could write something along the lines of:

> It is not clear whether, during the course of his conversation with Leo Sprog, Mr Shark has explicitly named Mr Brick as he does not do so in the section of the conversation provided in the question. If Mr Shark has expressly named Mr Brick as the person he refers to as a 'hypocrite' and 'philanderer' then . . . However, if Mr Shark has not explicitly named Mr Brick during the conversation then . . .'

Second, you must be careful here not to invent facts that are not present, explicitly or by implication, in the question. So, for example, it would not be relevant to consider the position had Mr Shark made his accusations directly to Mr Brick, because this is not something that is present in the question, nor is it something that may be naturally inferred as a possibility.

5.3.8   Similar real-life cases

Sometimes, the facts of a problem question will appear to match, or be very similar to, a real-life case that you have studied. If this happens, you should be careful not to assume that the problem question and real-life case are identical. This is because it is likely that the question writer has included a fact in the question that differs from the real-life case in an important way. This is to allow you to recognise the significance of the difference and to demonstrate that you fully understand the case law and understand which aspects of the real-life case are significant for the outcome.

For example, consider the simple problem question in Figure 5.4.

Adam, the farmer, writes to Clare of Clare's Wool Shop on 1st September offering to sell her some 'surplus wool' at a 'discount price'. Adam's letter concludes: 'please call in to see me if you would like to take me up on that offer'. Clare is unable to call in and see Adam but she posts a letter to him on 3rd September stating that she 'would like to purchase all Adam's surplus wool as she already has a customer who she has promised it to'. The letter is lost in the post and does not arrive at Adam's farm until 8th September. However, after not hearing back from Clare for a week, Adam has already sold the wool to Joe's Jumpers.

Advise Clare as to whether she has a claim in contract.

Figure 5.4 Simple problem question

At first glance, the scenario described in this question seems very similar to that in the well-known contract law case *Adams v Lindsell* (1818) 1 B & Ald 681 – there is an offer to sell wool and an attempt to accept this offer by post. The question writer has even called one of the characters Adam! Given this, it would be easy to conclude that the answer here is the same as in *Adams v Lindsell*, and that the postal rule should apply, so that Clare accepted Adam's offer, and formed a contract, as soon as she posted the letter.

There is, though, a significant difference between the scenario in the above question and *Adams v Lindsell*, which your marker will expect you to recognise. In the real-life case, when making their offer, the defendants had stated 'receiving your answer in course of post', i.e. they made it clear that the offer could be accepted by the post. In the above question, Adam states that Clare can accept the offer by calling in and seeing him. That is, whereas the defendants in *Adams v Lindsell* had stated that their offer could be accepted by post, Adam has made it clear that his offer should be accepted in person, and so he should not be bound by the postal rule.

In short, where part of a problem question looks very similar to a real-life case, you should be cautious before assuming they are the same, and that the result in the real-life case should apply to the problem question.

5.4 FINAL WORDS

The advice given in this chapter should be read in conjunction with that given in the following chapters, particularly Chapters 6 and 7. Of course, some of the more time-consuming methods I have described to help you unpack a question would be unsuitable in an examination scenario, because of the constraints on time. You should, though, find that – even in examinations – the techniques I describe above will provide you with an insight into how you may ensure you fully understand, and so are able to fully answer, the question being asked.

Chapter 6

Answering coursework questions

In this chapter, you will learn:

- what lecturers are looking for when marking coursework;
- how you can make sure you answer the question;
- how to plan and structure your answer;
- the importance of reading a variety of materials to inform your work;
- about appropriate, formal and academic writing style;
- how to write and proofread your answer to ensure that it is error-free

6.1   INTRODUCTION

Coursework is likely to form a significant element of your degree. Indeed, along with exams, coursework is probably the type of assessment that law students most frequently encounter.

For the purposes of this chapter, coursework may be defined as a type of assessment where students submit an answer to a set question and where they are expected to research and write their answer away from the classroom, unsupervised and largely unaided (though lecturers may be prepared to clarify some points).

Generally speaking, there are two types of question that law students will be set as coursework: problem questions and essay questions.

As discussed in Chapter 5, problem questions typically take the form of a fictional scenario in which a series of events occurs and where the student is expected to provide legal advice to one or more of the parties in the scenario. Essay questions are typified by the student being given a proposition about the law that they are then asked to 'discuss', 'evaluate', 'critically analyse', etc.

Along with dissertations, coursework tasks are among the types of assessment that are most in the students' control. This is for a number of reasons:

- students know, and have plenty of time to think about, the question in advance of submitting an answer;
- students have the time to read for and prepare their answers;
- students can choose when and where they work on their answers and can find times and places that suit their preferences; and
- students have the time to polish and improve their answers as much as they are able.

In this way, coursework may be distinguished from, for instance:

- exams, where:
    - the questions are usually unknown (though seen exams, where the students see the questions in advance, are sometimes used);
    - students will be in a room, usually with many other students, where they have no control over the conditions, such as lighting, temperature, seating, noise levels, and so on;
    - students' performance may be affected by nerves; and
    - students have a limited time in which to answer the questions;
- presentations, where:
    - students' performance may be affected by nerves;
    - students have little or no control over the conditions (time, lighting, temperature, etc.) in which they give their presentation;
    - the markers may ask questions that the students did not know in advance; and
    - students may be subject to interruption by the markers.

It is because coursework is a type of assessment that is probably most in students' control that you, as a student, should see it as one of your primary chances to excel, to demonstrate that you are a serious student who deserves high marks. How you may best do this is the subject matter of this chapter.

I have written the word 'time' more than once in the last few paragraphs, and it is important that you realise that students produce the best coursework answers when they have taken the time to research, plan, write, proofread and improve their work. I have heard some students claim that they 'do [their] best work' when they begin it the night before they have to submit. These students are not being honest with themselves (as I do not hesitate to tell them) and are more than likely attempting to legitimise the fact that they have not given themselves the space and time to produce the best work of which they are capable.

COMMON ERROR

Students who tell themselves, and others, that they produce their 'best work' when they start it the night before submission are not being honest with themselves. Producing a good answer to a coursework question requires you to give yourself the time to properly research, plan, write, proofread and improve your work.

6.2   WHAT MARKERS ARE LOOKING FOR (AND WHAT THIS MEANS FOR YOU)

Generally speaking, when marking students' work, lecturers will rely on two things: indicative marking criteria and their own sense of what amounts to, say, first-class work, upper-second-class (i.e. 2:1) work, lower-second-class (i.e. 2:2) work, and so on.

The indicative marking criteria will be produced by the institution or department in which you are studying. It is likely to be available to you and may be supplied at the start of your degree with the rest of the information you receive. The criteria indicate the characteristics a piece of work should possess to achieve a particular mark, and Table 6.1 shows what they may typically look like.

You will notice that the criteria are drafted in very broad terms. This is out of necessity; they cannot be too prescriptive, because they have to apply to a diverse range of answers to a diverse range of assessments. Markers, therefore, also have to employ their academic judgment when marking, i.e. their inherent sense of what is required for a particular mark. This will be drawn from the lecturers' experiences: as students themselves, as markers of student work, as second markers of colleagues' marking and as external examiners.

Also, when marking students' work, a lecturer will have in mind that the mark they give for a particular coursework may need to be confirmed by the second marker

Table 6.1 Indicative marking criteria

Level of performance	% mark	Criteria (undergraduate level 4)
Outstanding	90–100	Outstanding breadth and depth of knowledge, resulting in an excellent understanding of the principles of the subject, combined with the ability to: • analyse and synthesise knowledge from a range of appropriate sources; • apply theory in a practical context; • develop an argument that is well structured, clearly justified, and relevant to the particular circumstances of the situation or task in hand; • make excellent use of literature to support and justify the views expressed
Excellent	80–89	Real understanding of the principles of the subject, combined with the ability to: • analyse and synthesise knowledge from a range of appropriate sources; • develop an argument that is well structured, clearly justified, and relevant to the particular circumstances of the situation or task in hand; • make good use of literature, to support and justify the views expressed.
Very good	70–79	Sound understanding of the principles of the subject, with good depth and breadth of underpinning knowledge, combined with the ability to: • compare and contrast information obtained from a range of appropriate sources; • analyse and evaluate; • apply knowledge to specific scenarios in an appropriate manner; • develop an argument that is relevant to the particular circumstances of the situation or task in hand; • make effective use of literature from appropriate sources, to support the views expressed.

Table 6.1 continued

Level of performance	% mark	Criteria (undergraduate level 4)
Good	60–69	Understanding of the principles of the subject, with evidence of a reasonable depth of knowledge, combined with the ability to: • analyse and evaluate; • discuss the application of theory to practice; • structure argument in a logical manner; • make credible use of literature from appropriate sources, to support the views expressed.
Fair	50–59	Reasonable understanding of the principles of the subject, combined with the ability to identify key themes/principles. However, there may be: • little evidence of the ability to evaluate; • a lack of ability to develop a well-structured argument that is sufficiently focused on the task in hand; • some illogical structure; • some repetition; • limited evidence of reading (relies primarily on textbooks or other general sources).
Adequate	40–49	Understanding of the basic themes/principles, but lacks breadth of knowledge, focusing primarily on a description of theory. There may be: • problems with analysis and/or application of knowledge to the task in hand; • poor structuring and presentation; • little evidence of reading from appropriate sources.
Unsatisfactory	30–39	Only partial understanding of the basic themes/principles. The work addresses some of the obvious features of the task, but fails to reach the required standard. There may be: • difficulties in applying knowledge to the task in hand; • poor structuring and presentation; • limited outline of theory only; • little evidence of relevant reading.

Table 6.1 continued

Level of performance	% mark	Criteria (undergraduate level 4)
Poor	20–29	Inadequate and inaccurate knowledge displayed; limited effort and planning evident. There may be: • real difficulties in applying knowledge to the task in hand; • no evidence of relevant reading.
Very poor	10–19	Virtually no relevant knowledge displayed; little attempt to address the task in hand. There may be: • real weaknesses in structuring and presentation; • no evidence of reading.
Extremely poor	1–9	Totally inadequate attempt; virtually no relevant knowledge displayed. There may be: • no true attempt to address the task in hand; • no true effort to learn.
No attempt	0	

Source: Department of Law and Criminology, Edge Hill University

or external examiner (the roles of second markers and external examiners are explained in Chapter 1). Because of this, a marker will want to be able to justify – to either the second marker or external examiner – the mark they have awarded. What this means for you as a student is that you should do all that you possibly can to ensure that the first marker can award you a high mark, without fear of it being questioned by the second marker or the external examiner.

That is, you should do all that you can to ensure that you:

- answer the question as fully as possible;
- write and present your work as well as possible;
- fully and correctly reference your work; and
- demonstrate that you have engaged with a variety of materials (law reports, textbooks, journal articles, etc.) to inform your work.

Let's look at some lecturers' comments about what they look for when marking coursework.

LECTURERS' THOUGHTS	
What do you look for when marking coursework?	
Anna	'When marking coursework, I ask myself four basic questions: 1 Has the student answered the question? 2 Does the student know what they are talking about? 3 Have they put the effort in? 4 Is it well written, well presented and correctly referenced?'
Bill	'Content – does the student have the subject knowledge and is there appropriate coverage of the relevant issues and pertinent cases? Are the referencing and bibliography correct? Writing – in terms of structure, grammar and punctuation.'
Carol	'First, I look for content, the legal argument, have students identified what the question is about? The introduction is a good indicator here. With problem questions, I look, particularly, at application [of the law] and being relevant. Grammar is important because it indicates the grade [that should be given]. I would not [directly] penalise [for poor grammar], but it affects my overall judgment.'
David	'I look for the overall coherence of the written argument. I also look for the degree of support from either statute, case law or relevant academic commentary. The tone – is there a consistent academic tone with the avoidance of contractions or colloquialisms? I also look at the clarity and correctness of the footnotes and the referencing.'

I will draw on these comments in other parts of this chapter, but it is worth highlighting some initial points now.

Content

Each of the four markers quoted in Lecturers' Thoughts Box makes an evaluation of the content of the answers that they mark:

* whether the student has answered the question asked;
* whether their answer demonstrates good subject knowledge; and
* whether their answer addresses the pertinent issues.

Presentation

Each of the markers also makes reference to the presentation of the work:

* the quality of the writing, including the grammar and punctuation;
* the structure or overall coherence; and
* the referencing (see Chapter 11 for advice about referencing).

By 'presentation of the work', I mean that it should be well written and correctly referenced. I do not mean that it should contain unnecessary features that you have spent a long time producing, such as a fancy front page.

COMMON ERROR

Your marker will probably not appreciate the inclusion in your work of unnecessary features, such as a fancy front page, which add nothing of substance.

To explain, your marker will not want you to submit work that is badly scrawled on crumpled pieces of paper; however, they probably will not want you to waste your time on unnecessary gimmickry.

Of course, your work should look good on the page, but you can achieve this by presenting it plainly and simply. Anything else looks like you are trying to rely on style over substance, which leads to the suspicion that your work actually *lacks* substance. Indeed, your marker may ask whether you have spent time fancifying your work to hide a lack of content.

LECTURERS' PET HATES

'It really frustrates me when I feel like a student has spent a lot of time prioritizing style over substance. For example, students often erroneously think it is impressive to provide superfluous and useless additions to their essay, such as separate and fancy coversheet, contents pages for short essays, unnecessary graphics, graphs, charts and so on. It always makes me feel like the student thinks I will be impressed by their amount of efforts, when in actual fact, I see this as time wasting and not paying enough attention to what really matters in terms of getting good marks, i.e.: strong content and structure which fully addresses the question'.

Similarly, unless your lecturer has indicated otherwise, you should not submit your work in a folder purchased specially for it. Again, the use of such a specially purchased folder suggests a prioritising of style over content.

The following sections will discuss how you may ensure both the content and presentation of your work is correct. For now, it is worth noting that markers make a judgement on your work that depends, in part, on how well it is written and referenced. The reasons for this are not hard to understand: from the lecturer's perspective, it is relatively easy for students to make sure their work is well written and correctly referenced, and so, when students get this wrong, it suggests a lack of care and effort on their part.

Moreover, imagine that, while marking your work, your lecturer thinks it may be a borderline first-class piece of work: that it deserves either a high 2:1 or a low first-class mark, but that they are struggling to decide which. If the work is littered with presentational flaws – such as poor referencing or grammatical errors – the lecturer may conclude that, for these reasons, a first-class mark would not be appropriate. In fact, if the work is not free of presentational errors, a marker may think that they would struggle to justify a first-class mark to the second marker or external examiner and so decide that it is better to play it safe and award a 2:1 mark.

LECTURERS' PET HATES

'I hate it when students don't follow instructions such as that work must be in font size 12, double-spaced and justified.'

Getting the presentation of your work correct can be tiresome and laborious, but it is not difficult, and you should ensure that you do as much as you can to get this right, not least because it may make the difference between a first-class mark and a 2:1, between a 2:1 and a 2:2, and so on.

6.3   ANSWERING (AND NOT ANSWERING) THE QUESTION

Three of the lecturers quoted in the previous section mentioned, directly or indirectly, that they ask themselves whether the student has answered the question. You might think that it is so obvious that students should answer the assignment question that it should not need saying, yet students often do not do this.

For instance, look at the following question:

> The concepts of offer, acceptance and consideration are increasingly irrelevant in the modern law of contract.
>
> Discuss

Some students will read this and decide to write all that they know about offer, acceptance and consideration, or (much, much worse) all that they know about contract law.

This is strange behaviour indeed. The same students would not give such a non-answer in other areas of their life:

- If asked whether they wanted a cup of tea, they would not respond by giving a description of tea.
- If asked whether they thought a new nightclub was worth a visit, they would not answer by giving a brief account of UK nightclubs since the Second World War.
- A lawyer, when asked to outline their client's defence to a charge of murder, would be given very short shrift by the court if they proceeded to give an account of the law of homicide, or the criminal law in general.

Writing all that you know about a particular topic, regardless of whether it directly addresses the question, is sometimes known as the 'dumper-truck approach' (because students dump all they know about a topic on to the paper). It suggests that you cannot distinguish the relevant from the irrelevant, and you will be marked accordingly.

TIP BOX

It is unlikely that you are ever going to be asked to write all that you know about a particular topic so you should start with the assumption that you should not do it.

So, students need to ensure that all that they write is relevant to the question asked. They must also make sure that what they write is not too general.

LECTURERS' PET HATES

'I hate irrelevance, for example [a student writing] "This is a question about land law" and then they go on to explain what land law is. [This] kind of irrelevant sloppiness . . . shows sloppy thinking.'

The problem here is not simply that a general description of, say, land law is not directly relevant to the question asked; it is also that it is too broad and basic. As a student, you have to assume that your reader has a good basic understanding, so that you can – from the start of your answer – directly address the question asked, rather than waste space describing the irrelevant.

The issue of relevance in your answer is crucial. Students will sometimes take the dumper-truck approach because it is easier than thinking about the question and working out what they are being asked. It may also feel safer to write all that they know.

COMMON ERROR

Rather than directly answering the question, and ensuring that all that they write is relevant, students often write all that they know about a particular topic.

Also, because they want to demonstrate that they understand, students will sometimes include things in their answers that are not strictly relevant. This is a mistake. As a student, you need to be able to demonstrate the breadth and depth of your knowledge, while ensuring that all that you write addresses the question. This means that you should be prepared to exclude or remove material from your answer that is not directly relevant to the question asked.

WORK SMARTER

In answers to all types of assessment question, do not include material just to demonstrate that you understand it. If it is not relevant to the question asked – and you cannot make it relevant (without shoehorning it in) – then you should exclude it. Any other approach suggests that you cannot differentiate between the relevant and irrelevant.

There is a greater danger of not answering the question with essay questions than problem questions. This is because problem questions implicitly, and by their nature, tend to give more direction as to what is required to answer them, because what is required is (usually) advice about the various parts of the fictional scenario that make up the question. Even here, though, students occasionally take a dumper-truck approach for all or part of their answer.

TIP BOX

When answering a coursework question, ask yourself, honestly, at each stage – during the planning, writing and proofreading – whether all that you write is relevant and addresses the question.

6.4 PLANNING AND WRITING YOUR ANSWER

Whether you are answering an essay question or a problem question, I cannot stress enough how important it is for you to plan your answer, and you should spend a significant amount of time doing this.

I am sure that there are people in the world who can simply sit down and write a brilliant answer without taking the time to map it out on paper beforehand, but you should assume that you are not one of them.

6.4.1   Why plan?

Taking the time and effort to plan your answer is important for a number of reasons. First, it allows your thoughts, and the way you express them, to develop and mature. It gives you time to reflect on, and cultivate, your ideas and to write them in a way that perfectly captures what it is you want to express.

Second, planning your work will allow you to decide the best way to structure it. You should organise the different parts of your work so that they fit together to form a coherent, readable whole that demonstrates to your marker the depth, breadth and clarity of your understanding.

It's worth reminding you here of the thoughts of two of the lecturers, noted in Section 6.2 above: when marking, Bill and David look at the structure or overall coherence of the work – see Lecturers' Thoughts Box.

	LECTURERS' THOUGHTS
Bill	'[I look at the] Writing – in terms of *structure*, grammar and punctuation.'
David	'I look for the *overall coherence* of the written argument.'

All markers will make an evaluation of the structure and coherence of students' work. Remember, your reader – who will be your marker – should not have to try to disentangle your random thoughts that you have assembled in any old order. Rather, you should attempt to present your arguments as clearly and convincingly as possible, and good planning will enable you to do this.

Third, planning your work allows you to divide the production of it into stages. This, in turn, may help to alleviate writer's block, the phenomenon of sitting in front of a computer screen not knowing where to begin or what to write. It is worth acknowledging here that beginning the writing process is often quite hard (which is why, I suspect, many students delay starting writing their coursework), and, when one is trying to write, tasks that would usually seem an incredible chore – such as washing the dishes, ironing clothes or cleaning the bathroom – seem much more attractive alternatives than starting to type. Adopting the staged approach I describe below, or one like it, means that you divide the job of producing your coursework into more digestible chunks and you ease yourself into the writing process. Moreover, as you will see, using a staged approach will allow you to enrich your work at each step with added information, such as, for instance, academic opinion, judicial comments, etc.

6.4.2   How to plan your work

When planning any significant writing, I adopt the following approach. It is designed to systematically move me from capturing my initial thoughts, through producing a detailed plan, to writing the work; it also allows me to inform my work at each stage with the relevant primary and secondary material. As it happens, the method I describe is the one I have adopted when writing this book, so you can judge for yourself how effective it is (though, if you are reading this and thinking that it is not very well written, you probably need to read it again to appreciate the subtlety and sophistication of my prose style; if, on the other hand, you are reading this and thinking that it is very well written, then well done for being able to appreciate the subtlety and sophistication of my prose style).

It may be that you have your own method of planning and writing (or that you adapt the one I describe) that works better for you than mine. That is fine and absolutely appropriate. But, whichever method you employ, bear in mind the benefit of approaching your work in a systematic way, in stages, with each stage being used to crystallise your thoughts and move them to a more organised, well-structured state.

In brief, the method of planning and writing that I employ has the following steps:

- I begin by noting my initial thoughts on a blank piece of paper.
- I then read a little and add to my initial thoughts (and, in fact, I continue with this cyclical approach of planning and reading throughout each of the stages).
- Next, on another blank piece of paper, I organise my initial thoughts into a more ordered plan in the form of a spider diagram.
- I then begin to convert my diagrammatic plan into something more linear by writing it by hand (this also serves as an early written draft of my work).
- Finally, I type up my handwritten notes, making changes and improvements as I do so.

In order to demonstrate more fully how the method I use operates, I will imagine that I am answering the essay question in Box 6.1.

Box 6.1

The United Kingdom has a constitution.

Discuss.

Before you begin any planning, you must ensure that you fully understand the question: see Chapter 5 for advice on understanding essay and problem questions.

First stage

When planning my work, I begin with a blank, unlined sheet of paper. In fact, I have some pads of very large paper that I use for planning my work: a pad of A3 paper (i.e. 297 × 420 mm) and a pad of A2 (i.e. 420 × 594 mm). You can usually buy pads of this size in art shops.

I start by noting my initial thoughts, fairly randomly, on the paper. I don't worry too much about organising my initial thoughts at this stage, because this first stage is a brainstorming one, designed to capture my early ideas, and it is more important simply to get them on to the paper. I may, though, draw any links or make any associations that I think are present. So, at this first stage, I produce something that looks like Figure 6.1 (don't worry too much about being able to read the detail of the diagram; its purpose is simply to demonstrate what my plan looks like at this stage).

Second stage

I next engage in some initial reading, perhaps of the relevant pages of my textbooks, and note any further thoughts on the paper. In fact, I continue with the cyclical process of planning (or, even, writing) and reading during each stage of the work, and I find that this helps me to build a well-informed piece of work that has depth and nuance.

You may be tempted to think that it would be beneficial to undertake all the reading that you intend to do before you begin planning or writing your work. However (and you need to be honest with yourself about this), it may be that you are reading more and more to delay beginning one of the most difficult tasks:

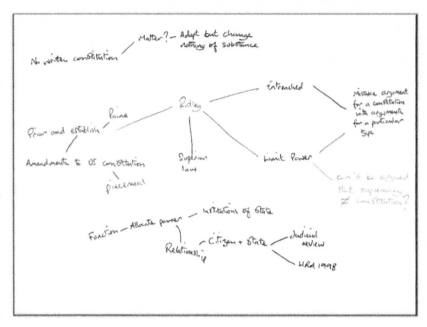

Figure 6.1 Notes from first planning stage

getting your thoughts down on paper. Moreover, interspersing your reading with planning/writing gives your reading more context, and, consequently, you are able to take more from it. That is, your reading will be more focused on answering the coursework question, and you can use it to make directly relevant points, because you are not reading in the abstract but, rather, against a background that you are creating and updating.

This reading and planning cycle helps me develop and add to my initial thoughts to produce something that looks like Figure 6.2.

Once I feel that I have enough material to begin to organise my work into something that is more structured, I move on to the third stage.

Third stage

This involves a second sheet of blank paper on which I arrange my ideas from the first sheet into a spider diagram: see Figure 6.3.

This allows me to impose more structure on my work, to start giving it shape and to group connected ideas together. For instance, if I enlarge a segment of the

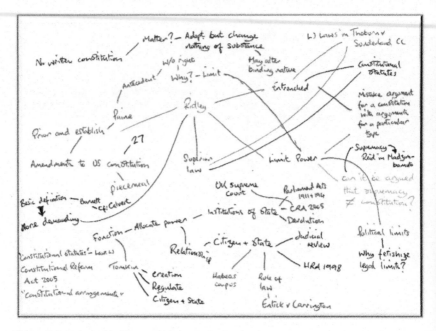

Figure 6.2 Notes added in second stage

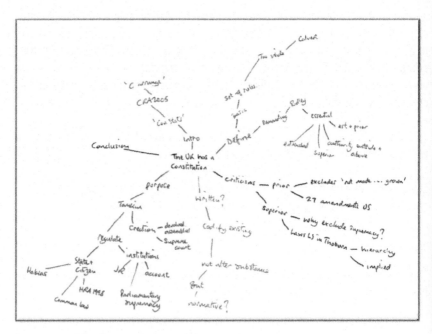

Figure 6.3 Spider diagram of arranged ideas

above spider plan, you can see that it deals with definitions of a constitution and compares a basic definition with something a little more demanding: see Figure 6.4.

It is worth repeating that you should continue to intersperse your planning with reading and use this reading to continue to develop your work.

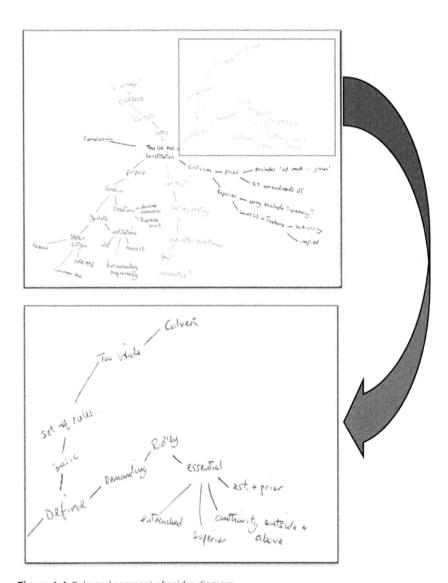

Figure 6.4 Enlarged segment of spider diagram

Fourth stage

This stage involves me changing my work into a more linear form; that is, to something that looks more like an essay than a diagram. Here, I write – by hand – my ideas as planned out in the spider diagram.

So, taking the selected section of the above spider plan as an example, I would write it as shown in Figure 6.5.

You will see that I write each new sentence, or new point, on a fresh line and that each sentence is separated by a line. This allows me to make amendments or to insert new ideas that I may think of after beginning writing. As a result of these amendments, I often end up with a hand-written version of my work that looks like Figure 6.6.

As noted above, this hand-written stage acts as an early written draft of my work that I then improve in the next stage.

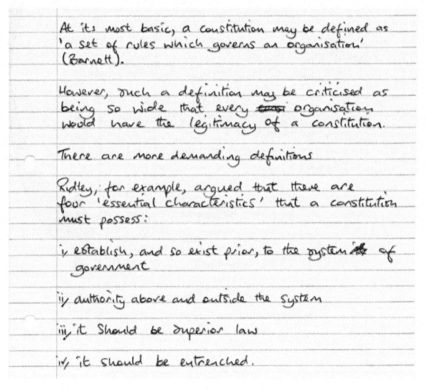

At its most basic, a constitution may be defined as 'a set of rules which governs an organisation' (Barnett).

However, such a definition may be criticised as being so wide that every organisation would have the legitimacy of a constitution.

There are more demanding definitions

Ridley, for example, argued that there are four 'essential characteristics' that a constitution must possess:

i) establish, and so exist prior, to the system of government

ii) authority above and outside the system

iii) it should be superior law

iv) it should be entrenched.

Figure 6.5 Ideas from spider diagram in linear form

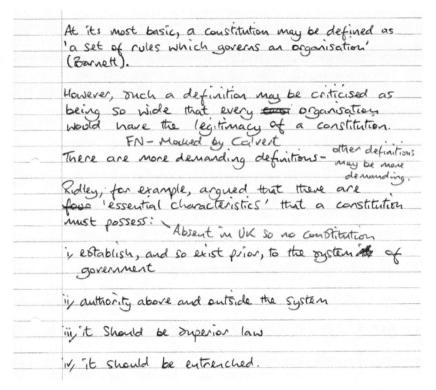

At its most basic, a constitution may be defined as
'a set of rules which governs an organisation'
(Barnett).

However, such a definition may be criticised as
being so wide that every ~~one~~ organisation
would have the legitimacy of a constitution.
    FN — Marked by Calvert
There are more demanding definitions — other definitions
                                        may be more
                                        demanding.
Ridley, for example, argued that there are
~~four~~ 'essential characteristics' that a constitution
must possess:
                    Absent in UK so no constitution
i, establish, and so exist prior, to the system ~~the~~ of
    government

ii, authority above and outside the system

iii, it should be superior law

iv, it should be entrenched.

Figure 6.6 Version with amendments

Fifth stage

At this stage, I begin typing up the essay. This will form the second draft of my
essay. It is important to note that I am not simply typing my hand-written work
verbatim. Rather, I may think of a better way to phrase a particular sentence, or I
may include a new argument or idea. So, the section of the coursework that I have
been working on in the above examples may read as shown in Box 6.2 at this
stage.

The above method works for me and it helps me to progress my initial thoughts,
via a number of steps, to a well-informed, well-structured early draft of work. As
noted above, you may adopt or adapt my method or employ one of your own
devising. Indeed, I urge you to give some honest thought to what works best for
you, and this might involve your experimenting with different approaches (I write
'honest thought' because some students will attempt to convince themselves that
what works best is to begin their coursework the night before it is due to be

---

Box 6.2

At its most basic, a constitution may be defined as 'a set of rules that governs an organisation'. Such a definition could be criticised, however, as being so wide that it confers the legitimacy of having a constitution on any organisation.[2] Other definitions may be more demanding. For instance, Ridley has stated that there are 'essential characteristics' that a constitution should have: it should establish the system of government and thus be prior to it; it should be an authority outside and above that which it establishes; it should be a form of superior law; and it should be entrenched.[3] He argues that, as these characteristics are absent in the United Kingdom, it cannot be considered to have a constitution.

---

submitted and to write it without a plan; as I indicate above, those who conclude that this is the best method for them are highly likely to be deluding themselves). Whatever your approach, I suggest that it should be such to enable you to move, systematically, from not knowing where or how to begin to actually writing the first draft of your coursework.

Moreover, I should note that, although the cyclical method of planning/writing and reading works for many people (and I urge you to try it), some find that it is not the best for them. For example, one of my colleagues, who produces fantastically sophisticated work, prefers to read all the relevant literature, then plan her work using a spider plan, and then write her work. I marvel at her intellectual ability to read, and keep in mind, all that is necessary, but I ask you to note that she still has a system that involves her planning her work and that has different stages that are used to help her crystallise her thoughts. Also, although my colleague is able to produce excellent work in this way, she is a very experienced academic, and, as I noted above, for most people, reading everything before starting would simply be a way of delaying planning or writing.

6.5   READING AND INDEPENDENT THOUGHT

Throughout Section 6.4.2, I have suggested that your planning and initial writing should be interspersed with reading relevant material. I describe the different types of reading matter that you should engage with in Chapter 3, and you should read over that chapter to understand the different types of primary and secondary sources available to you. Here, I simply wish to reiterate the importance of drawing on different sources to inform your work and help you produce work that demonstrates independent thought.

One of the errors students often make when writing coursework is that they forget that they have brains of their own and the capacity to think for themselves. They often produce coursework that simply regurgitates their lecturer's arguments, or those made by other academics, without the work containing any critique or thoughts of their own. Adopting such an approach may get you a pass mark, but it will not get the higher marks that you should be aiming for. You should note, here, the comments I once read by an external examiner: 'Parrots don't understand, they repeat, and parrots don't get first class law degrees'.

COMMON ERROR

An error commonly made by students is to simply regurgitate the relevant lecture in their coursework or exam. This is a mistake for a number of reasons. First, it may not answer the question because it may be an instance of the dumper-truck approach mentioned above. Second, even the most narcissistic lecturer will find it tiresome to have their own ideas repeated back to them. Finally, the marker will read answer after answer that simply regurgitates the lecture and, for that reason, none of them will stand out as deserving high marks; indeed, repeating the lecture in essay form is the hallmark of the poor to average student.

Better students do not simply recycle others' ideas. Rather, their work contains their own informed, independent arguments. This is especially the case in answers to essay questions where you are expected to critically discuss, assess or evaluate a particular proposition. However, even in problem questions, you should take the opportunity to demonstrate some independent thought if possible.

If you produce coursework that contains your own informed, independent arguments, then you are more likely to be producing work that contains elements not always found in undergraduate work, and, for this reason, your work is more likely to get good marks.

I should be clear what I mean about making use of your own independent arguments. Your academic claims are capable of being as valid as anyone else's – those of your fellow students, your lecturers or Professor Fantastic from Wonderful

University. However, that does not mean that you should feel free to write uninformed (or ill-informed), immoderate and unsubstantiated assertions. Remember, when writing any work for your degree – whether coursework or exam – you are not writing for a tabloid newspaper. Rather, you should be trying to write a scholarly, academic, informed piece of work.

COMMON ERROR

Do not write like you are the editor of a tabloid newspaper. An assertion such as 'The Great British Constitution is the best in the world!' has no place in an academic piece of work.

It is worth writing here that you should also be cautious about making any sweeping assertions in your work. It may be tempting to write that 'all judges are white, middle class and male', but it is manifestly untrue, and it is probably true of all such sweeping assertions (including this one) that they are too simplistic and so lack the nuance that you should be aiming for with your work.

I should also point out that your independent arguments do not need to be world changing or incredibly original. They simply need to be sufficient to demonstrate to your marker that you are able to produce work that contains informed, independent opinion.

I have used the word 'informed' a number of times in this section. This is deliberate. I am trying to emphasise that you must undertake a significant amount of reading to inform yourself of the different, relevant academic arguments that exist. This will achieve a number of things. It will expose you to a variety of viewpoints that will help you to produce nuanced, sophisticated work. It will also mean that you see the different types of academic argument that are posited, as well as how they are made, and this will give you a better understanding of the types of argument that you could make in your work. That is, by acquainting yourself with the scholarly arguments deployed by others, you are better equipping yourself to make your own.

Reading a variety of material, though, does more than simply inform your work and teach you how to make academic contentions. If you draw on, and (importantly) make reference to, a number of different materials, then you indicate to your marker that you have put some effort into doing your work, and they will wish to reward that effort. To illustrate, if your coursework makes reference to only one textbook, then you might as well write across your answer that you cannot be bothered to do much work, because that is what your marker will take it to mean, and they will mark you accordingly.

Indeed, with essay questions, it is usually particularly appropriate to make reference to, and critically evaluate, various pertinent academic opinions; in fact, the question may positively require you to do this.

The same is less true of problem questions. These are more practical in nature and are designed to get you to demonstrate your understanding of the law in an applied way. Given this, it would not be appropriate to engage in lengthy discourse about the various academic opinions that exist.

That is not to say that academic opinion is not relevant when answering problem questions and that you should not make use of it. In answering such questions, you will still want to demonstrate the breadth of your reading and understanding to your marker. However, you need to do this in a way that does not detrimentally affect the relevance of your answer. That is, your use of academic commentary should not normally be as extensive in answers to problem questions as it is in answers to essay questions. Rather, mention of such commentary should be just enough to demonstrate to your marker that you are aware that there is such commentary out there, or that a particular point of law has been disputed by academics, without making a substantial departure from directly addressing the issues in the question.

For instance, with regard to a defamation problem question (such as the one in Section 5.3 of Chapter 5), it may be that some academics have discussed whether newspapers reporting an accusation made against a politician should be liable in defamation. If so, it would be useful to make a brief mention of this. You could do so directly in the text. Alternatively, you could include a short footnote that reads: 'For an alternative view, see: Professor Smartypants "Qualified privilege in political reporting" [2005] Defamation LR 220, 226'.

You should, though, be careful when using footnotes in this way; if you do it too much, your marker may think you are attempting to use footnotes to circumvent the word limit and penalise you accordingly. (I should say that Professor Smartypants, his article and the Defamation Law Review, are fictional, though you will certainly meet some smartypant professors in the course of your degree.)

Academic commentary may also be useful and pertinent in problem questions if the legal position with regard to a part of the question is unclear and has been subject to academic discussion. Such 'grey' areas are often used by lecturers when setting questions to allow you to demonstrate that you are aware that the law on a particular point is not settled, and that there are different opinions on the matter (see Section 5.3.5 in Chapter 5).

Where this is the case, it is likely that your lecturer will have made reference to this ambiguity in their classes (which is one of the reasons it is so important to attend all classes – see Chapter 2). In such a situation, it is not only appropriate, it is probably necessary, that you give a brief account of the different opinions available by making reference to the academic literature.

Extensive reading of a variety of materials is important for a further reason when answering both essay and problem questions: it will demonstrate to your marker that you have the intellectual capability to understand, and make use of, different, sometimes conflicting, arguments.

WORK SMARTER

You must read a variety of materials to inform your work and, to get the better marks, you should demonstrate the extent and breadth of your reading in your references and footnotes.

I should add a note of warning here. Do not attempt to claim that you have read something when you haven't to make it appear as though you have engaged in more reading than you have. Your marker will know from the quality of your work whether you have read all that you claim and they will not appreciate any attempt to fool them.

As for what types of material you should use to inform your work, you should draw on a mix of sources, both primary (e.g. legislation and law reports) and secondary (e.g. textbooks and journal articles). What the balance should be between primary and secondary materials depends on the nature of the question you are answering.

You should make use of a variety of textbooks and academic articles to inform your work; the more you use, the better your work, and your mark, will be. You might also consider making appropriate use of monographs. (Refer to Chapter 3 for an explanation of these different types of reading material.)

When making use of textbooks, be aware that some are more suitable than others to be used as a source for your work. For example, the small, accessible, exam-revision-type books that are available may be excellent to help you understand, but you should not make reference to them as a source that you have relied on when writing your coursework.

You should also be careful when making use of, and making reference to, websites. There are some excellent academic blogs and websites on the Internet. Most, though, are not suitable as academic sources on which you may draw to inform your work. Moreover, if your work primarily draws on sources from the World Wide Web, then you may be giving your marker an impression that you do not want: that you cannot be bothered reading anything more substantial, such as textbooks, journal articles or monographs. You may also create the impression that you started your coursework the night before it had to be submitted, because your marker may assume that the reason you have relied on the web so heavily is that you did not leave yourself enough time to make use of more substantive sources and have simply accessed the easiest available source. That is, you may create the impression that the coursework is not the result of much effort on your part.

To be clear, in advising you not to rely too much, if at all, on sources available on the World Wide Web, I am not referring to the journal articles, law reports and legislation that you can access via legal databases such as Westlaw or LexisNexis. Rather, I am referring to web content that is generally and freely available.

6.6   WRITING STYLE AND STRUCTURE

Your coursework should be structured and written so that it conveys your ideas and arguments to your reader (i.e. your marker) as clearly as possible. To state the matter bluntly, even if you develop the most brilliant and original arguments, you will not receive good marks if your marker cannot make sense of them because of the way your work is written or structured. Remember, your lecturers are time-poor – particularly when marking tens, or even hundreds, of coursework answers – and they will not have the time to try and decipher something that lacks clarity because it is badly written or structured. Also, keep in mind that language is the tool of lawyers, and, as a law student, you need to be able to explain complicated ideas in an intelligible way. Indeed, whether you go on to practise as a lawyer, or enter some other profession, the ability to communicate complicated ideas in a way that makes sense to your audience will be a valuable asset.

In all your writing, you should try to see things from the perspective of your would-be reader and make sure that your writing is not so dense, or your structure so complicated, that they will get lost. This is a matter of judgment: you need to write in such a way that your reader can make sense of it, using a clear prose style and signposting to your reader where you are taking them; however, you should avoid overdoing it so that your work appears laboured. As with all matters of judgment, you will become better at it with more experience, both of others' work (e.g. by reading textbooks, journal articles and the like) and through your own work.

6.6.1 Word limits and answer length

Most, if not all, coursework questions will specify a word limit – the maximum number of words that you may take to answer the question. There may be a rule whereby you are permitted to exceed this word limit; for example, that you can go up to 10 per cent over the word limit (we may refer to this as the absolute word limit). However, you should aim for your work to be as close to the word limit as possible and you should not exceed the absolute word limit – there may be penalties if you do.

Also, importantly, you should not be significantly below the word limit. If you are, it may be taken by your marker as evidence that your work lacks sufficient depth, analysis and detail.

Table 6.2 Word limits – what you need to know

1 What is the word limit for the coursework you are answering?
2 Are the footnotes and bibliography included or excluded? That is, are they included or excluded when calculating the words you have used?
3 Are you permitted to exceed the word limit without penalty, and, if so, by how much?
4 Is there a formal lower word limit, for example, that your work will be penalised if it is a certain percentage below the word limit?

COMMON ERROR

Ensure that your work does not fall significantly below the word limit. If it does, your marker may take it as evidence that it lacks sufficient content and mark it accordingly.

Most word-processing programs have a facility that enables you to ascertain the word length of your work.

COMMON ERROR

Often, you will be required to state the length of your work. Do not be tempted into dishonesty about this by claiming that your work is longer or shorter than it actually is. Your marker will have a good sense of what, say, a 2,000 word essay looks like and it is easy for them to check. Moreover, such dishonesty may infringe your institution's academic regulations and result in disciplinary action being taken against you.

6.6.2   Basic structure

At perhaps its most basic, your coursework should have three parts: an introduction, the main part and a conclusion. This is sometimes characterised as:

* tell them what you are going to tell them (the introduction);
* tell them (the main part); and
* tell them what you have told them (the conclusion).

6.6.2.1 The introduction

As the above suggests, your introduction should indicate to your reader, in broad terms, what they are about to read. In answers to essay questions, your introduction can also provide some context for your essay. See, for example, the introductory paragraph in Box 6.3, which is the start of the sample essay question 'The UK has a constitution. Discuss' (see Section 6.4.2, above).

You will see that the last sentence in the example paragraph in Box 6.3 performs the main function of the introduction: it informs the reader, in general terms, what they are about to read. Of course, for a longer essay, or one that has more substance, this part of the introduction would be longer and more detailed.

Yet, this introductory paragraph is doing more than simply indicating the content of the essay that follows; it also situates the question in a wider setting. Scene-setting in this way makes the start of the essay less jarring for the reader than it

---

Box 6.3

Recent years have seen the creation, and dissolution, of a Secretary and Department of State for Constitutional Affairs, the enactment of the Constitutional Reform Act 2005 and judicial statements that the United Kingdom has 'constitutional' statutes[1] and 'constitutional arrangements'.[2] Despite these developments, it would seem that the question of whether the United Kingdom has a constitution is one which has yet to receive a conclusive answer. In discussing this issue, two different ways of defining constitutions will be examined: by characteristics and by purpose.

---

would have been had I dived straight into the answer. It also demonstrates to the marker that I am able to site the question in a wider context.

You should take a different approach when answering problem questions. Again, your introduction to such questions should inform your reader, in broad terms, what they are about to read. However, because problem questions usually require you to give advice about how the law would apply in practice – rather than enter into a discussion or engage in critique – it is not necessary to provide the wider context. Rather, you should move more directly to providing the advice required, and, in fact, your introduction for the answer to problem questions can be quite brief. So, Box 6.4 shows how an introduction to the defamation problem question given in Section 5.3 of Chapter 5 might read.

You would then proceed to give a definition of defamation, drawing on the appropriate authorities, before dealing with each of the issues raised in the question in turn.

When answering problem questions, in the introduction and elsewhere, unless it is necessary to make your point, you should not repeat the facts of the question or include material that is not necessary.

Box 6.4

Any legal claims that Mr Brick may have with regard to the scenario in the question would be in defamation. This is because, on the face of it, the various statements made about him are capable of harming his reputation.

LECTURERS' PET HATES

'My pet hate [when students are answering problem questions], is too much abstract discussion, too much recital of irrelevant factual information and reproducing [the facts of] the question in the answer.'

I have stated a number of times that the introduction for answers to both essay and problem questions should indicate what the reader is about to read, in broad, general terms. This is because you want your introduction to signpost what is to come; however, you do not want it to give too much away so that your work appears repetitive.

TIP BOX

When answering essay questions, the main function of the introduction is to indicate to the reader what they are about to read; for this reason, you should write the introduction last so that it accurately reflects what is written in your essay.

6.6.2.2 The conclusion

The conclusion should briefly summarize the arguments you have made, or the advice you have given, in the main part of your essay. As with the introduction, it should broadly state what has been argued, though it can and should be a little more detailed than the introduction. In addition, ideally, you should attempt to write it in a way that does not simply repeat what has been written in the main part of your work; you are obviously reiterating what you have written, so there will be some repetition in substance, but you should try to phrase it in a way so that it does not read as simple repetition.

Box 6.5 shows how a conclusion to the essay question 'The UK has a constitution. Discuss', given in Section 6.4.2, might read.

The conclusion for a problem question can be a simple summary of the advice given in the main part of the work. For instance, Box 6.6 shows a conclusion for the defamation problem question given in Chapter 5, Section 5.3.

Box 6.5

In discussing whether the United Kingdom has a constitution, the validity of identifying the existence of a constitution by reference to prescribed characteristics has been assessed. The position taken by Ridley, in particular, has been evaluated. His claim that certain characteristics are essential for a constitution to exist has been challenged. It has also been argued that it is a fallacy to conclude that the absence of a written constitution means that the United Kingdom cannot be considered to have a constitution, though codification might change the normative value of constitutional rules and the ease by which they may be altered. Finally, it has been argued that if one seeks to define a constitution by function, the United Kingdom's system of government performs the tasks that Tomkins, for one, states a constitution should perform. For this reason, it is suggested that one could conclude that the United Kingdom does indeed have a constitution.

Box 6.6

So, in summary, Mr Brick would be advised that he would have a claim in libel against Leo Sprog for the letter written by Mr Sprog to *The Ormsborough Star*. He may also have a claim in slander for the claims made about him by Barry Shark if he can demonstrate that they suggest he is unfit to carry out his profession as an MP. However, Mr Shark may be able to rely on the defence of truth with regard to his claim that Mr Brick is 'a philanderer'. Mr Brick would not have a claim in defamation for the statements made by Mr Sprog in the House of Commons because such statements are covered by absolute privilege.

6.6.2.3 Sentences and paragraphs

Your coursework answer should, of course, be divided into paragraphs; these are the building blocks of your essay. The purpose of paragraphs is to split your work into easily manageable chunks, to allow your reader to digest the information they are given. They introduce natural breaks into your written work, and, grammatically speaking, each new paragraph should deal with a new idea. Moreover, they should be logically sequenced so that each one naturally follows from the ones that preceded it.

Your paragraphs should not be overly long. If you end up with a very long paragraph, you should consider splitting it into two or more smaller ones. This is so even if the longer one deals with a single idea or argument. This will make your work easier to read and, for that reason, improve its clarity.

You should also avoid paragraphs that are too short. Strictly speaking, there is nothing grammatically incorrect with a paragraph that is, for instance, one sentence long. However, short paragraphs might make your work seem fragmentary, and so they are best avoided.

There is no rule governing the length of paragraphs: it is a matter of judgment, and you will be able to better make this judgment the more you read and the more you write. Having said that, as a (very rough) guide, if you are writing in font size 12, double-spaced text, then two or three paragraphs per side of A4 paper would be an appropriate length. If you find you have a paragraph that extends beyond one side of A4, then you should consider dividing it into smaller blocks.

As with paragraphs, your sentences should not be so long so that your reader loses the sense of what you are attempting to convey. This does not mean you should only use short sentences. You should aim for your work to contain a mix of short and longer sentences. This will make your work more interesting to read and will, therefore, better hold the attention of your reader.

6.6.3   Problem question structure and your answer

Students are often unclear about which order to deal with the different issues when answering problem questions. Generally speaking, when answering such questions, you should deal with each issue in turn, by which I mean you should identify the issue and what its legal significance is and, if appropriate, conclude your advice with regard to that issue, before moving on to the next.

Also, you can usually deal with the issues in the order that they arise in the question (I write 'usually' because, of course, two or more facts may be relevant in combination but be found in different parts of the question).

So, to take the defamation question in Section 5.3 of Chapter 5 as an example, you would begin with a short paragraph identifying the matter as one of defamation and, after an introductory definition of defamation, you can deal with the different issues in the order they arise in the question; for example:

- First, you can deal with the telephone conversation between Barry Shark and Leo Sprog, particularly, and in turn:
  - (a) with the fact that this is an issue of slander rather than libel and what that means for any potential claim by Arthur Brick;
  - (b) with the issue of publication – that the potentially defamatory statement has been made to a third party;
  - (c) with the fact that, given that Mr Shark does not appear to name Mr Brick (though, of course, he may have done in another part of the conversation), Mr Brick will have to rely on the rules of inference when making any claim against Mr Shark;
  - (d) with the fact that Mr Shark accuses Mr Brick of being a hypocrite and illustrates this by claiming that he has shares in Dodgy Housing plc and did not object to planning permission with regard to building work undertaken by them;
  - (e) with the fact that the claim with regard to the shares is untrue;
  - (f) with the fact that Mr Shark accuses Mr Brick of being a philanderer, and that this might be considered to be true and, if so, not defamatory.
- Second, you can deal with the statement made by Mr Sprog in the House of Commons and that this would be protected by parliamentary privilege.
- Third, you can deal with the letter from Mr Sprog to the local paper, which is unlikely to be protected by any kind of privilege.

6.6.4 Writing style

Your writing style should be such that it conveys your meaning as clearly as possible. For this reason, you should not adopt a flowery, convoluted prose style. Rather, a plain and simple style will best communicate your arguments.

Your writing style should also be formal, academic and scholarly. I have not adopted such a formal style when writing this book because I wanted to make it as engaging and easy to read as I could. However, if I were writing a more formal piece – say, a journal article or a monograph – then I would write in a more academic way.

Adopting a formal, academic style requires a number of things. In the first place, you should not use slang words or phrases. To illustrate, a few years ago, one of my students wrote in an essay: 'Separation of powers does exactly what it says on the tin'. Although I think I understood his meaning, the use of such a colloquial phrase is not appropriate in an academic essay.

Similarly, you should not engage in any kind of 'text-speak' – u prbly no wot I meen!!! (Apologies to my readers for my embarrassingly pathetic attempt to replicate a method of communicating that I'm much too old and un-cool to do with any sense of authenticity.) Rather, your work should be grammatically correct, and the words you use should be correctly spelled and written in full.

It is appropriate to use abbreviations at times; it is common, for example, to do this when writing about legislation, organisations or other things to which you repeatedly refer. But, you should write the thing out in full the first time you mention it, followed by its abbreviation in brackets to inform your reader of how you intend to refer to it in the remainder of your work. For example: 'At Prime Minister's Question Time (PMQs), the Leader of the Opposition challenged the Prime Minister on his lack of support for the Human Rights Act 1998 (HRA) . . .' However, you should only do this if you refer to the same thing quite often in your work.

The academic style also means that you should not use contractions. A contraction is a single word derived from two words, with absent letters being signified by an apostrophe. Although such contractions are useful in everyday speaking and writing, they are not appropriate in academic work and should be avoided.

COMMON ERROR

Do not use contractions in academic work.

Examples of contractions:

Can not ————— becomes ————— Can't

Will not ————— becomes ————— Won't

Have not ————— becomes ————— Haven't

WORK SMARTER

The best way to understand what the academic style requires is to read academic work, such as journal articles, and the judgments given in law reports.

Also, as an undergraduate, you should not write in the first person. That is, you should not write something like: '*I* think . . .', 'It is *my* contention that . . .' or 'It seems to *me* that . . .'

As it happens, there is an arguable case that there is nothing particularly un-academic or informal about writing in the first person. Indeed, many academics, including this one, adopt a first-person style at times, even in their academic works (articles and monographs). However, to be blunt, I can get away with it. As an undergraduate, you are likely to be in the position where most, if not all, of your lecturers believe that it is not appropriate to write in the first person, and, for that reason, you should not do it.

Avoiding writing in the first person leaves you with the problem of how you can express yourself in your coursework. The following examples might help to give you some ideas:

- 'Ridley's assertions may be criticised on a number of grounds . . .'
- 'Mr Brick should be advised . . .'
- 'It is submitted . . .'
- 'The author submits . . .'
- 'This essay will examine . . .'

I have two final points to make about writing style. First, try to avoid using more words than necessary – if you do, your prose will appear flabby, overwritten and laborious to wade through; if you use just the words necessary, your work will appear more direct and dynamic.

Second, when writing – whether you are writing an academic piece or writing an informal email to a friend – you should try to vary the language used; that is, you should be careful that your writing does not repeatedly use the same word (or a similar word), again and again, close together. If your writing does repeatedly use the same word, then what you write will jar with your reader, and your writing will appear repetitive and be a chore to read.

To illustrate, in the preceding paragraph, the word 'writing' appears seven times and the word 'write' once; 'repeatedly' is used twice and 'repetitive' once; and the words 'reader' and 'read' are used in the same sentence. The paragraph would be better if it was written as shown in Box 6.7.

You will note that, in the example in Box 6.7, I have not simply replaced repeated words: I have restructured the paragraph. Of course, it is not always possible to vary your language in this way, but you should avoid repetition where you can.

Box 6.7

Second, whether drafting an academic piece or an informal email to a friend, you should try to vary the language used; that is, you should be careful that you do not use the same word (or a similar word), again and again, close together. Such repetition will jar with your reader, and he or she will find it a chore to wade through your work.

TIP BOX

A thesaurus will help you vary the language you use in your work. These are available both online and in hard copy book form.

6.7 PROOFREADING AND IMPROVING YOUR WORK

LECTURERS' THOUGHTS

Heather	'I find that students don't properly proofread their work. These are people who want to be a lawyer – if they submitted stuff like that to a judge he would send it back unread and they would be hit with [an order for] costs.'

It would be difficult to over-emphasise the importance of proofreading your work to improve it. Remember, at least in part, your work will be assessed on how well it is written and presented, and effective proofreading can help you to ensure that this is as good as you can make it.

TIP BOX

Use the spell-check function on your word-processing programme to quickly scan your work to see if any misspelled words have been highlighted. Do not, though, allow the programme to automatically make changes because it may make alterations that you do not want.

Proofreading is not simply about eradicating errors. It is about polishing your work and ensuring not only that it is error free, but also that it is as well expressed and well structured as possible. Given this, you should consider proofreading to be an integral part of the writing process, rather than something you do five minutes before the deadline for submitting your work.

TIP BOX

When writing coursework, use the find function on your word-processing programme to look for words which you often misspell. For instance, if you commonly write 'statue' instead of 'statute' use the find function to see if the word 'statue' is in your work.

The best time to first proofread your work is when you have completed a typed draft to which you do not intend to make any significant changes. It would be ideal if you could have a gap of a day or so between finishing this draft and proofreading. This is because the time away from your work will mean that you are less familiar with it and are, therefore, more likely to spot any errors or changes that need to be made. I recognise, however, that such a gap may not be achievable.

WORK SMARTER

Remember, if you cannot understand what you have written, neither will your marker. When proofreading, if you cannot make full sense of something, you should change it to make it clearer.

The best way to proofread is to read your work aloud. Doing this will mean that you are less likely to skim over what you have written – which is a danger because of your familiarity with it. It also means that you will hear if something is not correct or is not phrased as well as it could be.

TIP BOX

The best way to proofread your work is to read it aloud. This will allow you to hear any mistakes and ensure that your work is as well-written as possible.

For any changes that you make, read over that part of the coursework again – and, if possible, the surrounding sentences and paragraphs – to make sure that you have not left any errors, and that your changes fit in with the adjacent text. If you make some significant changes, read over the whole work again to ensure that it is error free.

Chapter 7

Exams

This chapter will:

- discuss the different types of exam that you may encounter;
- consider the expectations of markers when marking exams;
- explain what you should find out about an exam before you sit it;
- discuss how you may best prepare for exams;
- discuss how to apportion time between, and how to answer, the questions in exams;
- consider some techniques for dealing with nerves.

7.1 INTRODUCTION

Along with coursework, examinations are probably the type of assessment that you are most likely to encounter as a law student.

Many, but not all, students dislike exams. This is for a number of understandable reasons, including:

- they may suffer from nerves, which may, in turn, affect their performance;
- they may believe that they do not do as well in exams as in other types of assessment such as coursework;
- the (usually) unknown aspect of exams – i.e. that you do not know the questions that will be asked – is often a source of anxiety;
- students may worry that they will forget important information;
- they may worry that they will not be able to write enough in the time permitted.

The advice in this chapter will, I hope, assuage any concerns that you may have about exams and help you make the best of them.

LECTURERS' THOUGHTS	
Anna	'It can become a self-fulfilling prophecy when a student believes they are bad at exams. It is much better to be open-minded and to reposition yourself as someone who is trying to get better at them rather than as someone who is not very good at them.'

7.2   EXAM TYPES AND CONFIGURATIONS

There are different types of exam, and Table 7.1 describes some of the common types and factors.

Table 7.1 Exam types and factors

Seen or unseen exams	A seen exam is one where the students have access to the exam paper before they sit it, for instance, a day or a week before. This allows them to prepare answers beforehand, which they will usually have to write from memory in the exam An unseen exam is one where the students do not see the paper before they sit it
Open- or closed-book exams	In open-book exams, students are permitted to take textbooks (as specified by the lecturer) or, sometimes, their notes into the exam to consult while sitting the paper. This is not permitted in closed-book exams
Statute books or other materials permitted	Sometimes students are allowed to take statute books or other materials into the exam to consult while sitting the paper. The particular statute book that is permitted may be specified by the lecturer
Compulsory elements	Many exams have a compulsory element. This might be, for example, that the students have to answer a particular question or questions; that they have to answer at least one question from each section of the paper; or that they have to answer at least one essay and one problem question
Reading time	Students are sometimes given reading time of, say, 10 or 15 minutes to read over the exam paper before they begin answering any questions. Students are sometimes permitted to make notes in this time

If you are permitted to take a statute book or textbook into the examination, you need to know, before the exam, whether these must be unmarked or whether you can, say, highlight some of the text or use page markers to help you quickly find relevant sections.

It almost goes without saying that you should find out as much as possible about the type and format of any exam long before you sit it.

7.3   MARKERS' EXPECTATIONS

Generally speaking, markers will be more lenient in some regards when marking exams than when marking coursework. That is, they will recognise that it is a pressured situation and will be more forgiving of grammatical, spelling or other types of error. They will not expect the same level of care to be taken over presentation in exams as in coursework.

66 99	**LECTURERS' THOUGHTS**
Eleanor	'I am more particular when marking coursework than exams. I'm more willing to forgive grammatical and other mistakes in exams than in coursework.'

Examiners will even accept some lapses of memory, say the name of a case, provided that you are able adequately to convey the case you mean – for instance, by description ('the snail in the bottle case') – and that you do not do it too often.

Moreover, you will not normally be required to provide the citation for a case, as you would in a piece of coursework, or – unless it is necessary for the point you are making – the year in which it was decided (though you should check with your lecturer what is required).

Exams are, inevitably, a test of memory to some extent. However, your marker will give more credit for evidence of a substantive understanding and application of the relevant law than for feats of memory. So, for instance, a marker will be more impressed by the fact that a student fully understands how Lord Atkin's opinion in *Donoghue v Stevenson* [1932] AC 562 applies to the exam question than a memorised verbatim quotation from the judgment.

WORK SMARTER

A marker will be more impressed by a full understanding and application of the relevant law than by huge chunks of text – whether from judgments, textbooks or some other source – remembered verbatim.

In addition, your marker will not give you much credit for an answer that you have written and learned before the exam and that you use, regardless of what the exam question asks.

LECTURERS' PET HATES

'My pet peeve is when it is obvious that a student has written an answer [before the exam], memorised it and is giving that as their answer no matter what the question is asking.'

For a similar reason, lecturers will not be impressed by an answer that is a simple regurgitation of their lecture. Indeed, as with coursework, one of the main causes of students not doing as well as they might in exams is that they fail to answer the question asked but, rather, take the dumper-truck approach (as described in Section 6.3 of Chapter 6): writing all they know about, say, the rule of law, rather than addressing the particular question asked.

LECTURERS' PET HATES

'One of my pet hates is students in exams writing out my lecture verbatim, as one of their answers. All that demonstrates is that they attended the lecture, made good notes and have the ability to remember them; we expect more than that.'

Finally, you should make sure that your answers are of sufficient length. So, for example, if you are required to answer three questions in a 2-hour exam, you should ensure that each question looks like 40 minutes' worth of work.

LECTURERS' PET HATES

'In exams, a failure to answer the question is a problem and I hate it when you get an exam [answer] book and an answer is just a paragraph long.'

7.4   BEFORE THE EXAM

In the lead-up to the exams, be sensible and do all that you can to keep yourself fit and well. Make sure that you eat well (by which I mean healthily) and get plenty of rest – do not have any 'all nighters' (either to work or party). Also, if you are able to exercise, bear in mind its benefits for relieving stress, boosting confidence and aiding concentration. You don't have to do much, even something like a walk can be very beneficial.

7.4.1   Things you need to know

There are some things you need to know in advance of the exam. Although these are fairly obvious, it is worthwhile me taking the time to spell them out.

You need to know:

- the time and venue of the exam – check and double-check this;
- the type of exam (e.g. whether seen or unseen, open or closed book, etc.);
- the number of questions on the exam and how many of these you need to answer;
- the weighting of each question: whether the questions are all worth equal marks, or some are worth more than others;
- the length of the exam (e.g. 2 hours);
- whether there are any compulsory requirements (for instance, that you must answer the first question, or one question from each section of the exam);
- whether there is any reading time for the exam, and, if so, whether you are permitted to make notes during this time.

You should get this information from official sources, rather than rely on your fellow students: ask your lecturers if need be.

Bear in mind that each exam may have its own rules, so that, for instance, you are permitted to take a statute book into the contract law exam but not into the public law exam; or, it may be that there is a compulsory question that you must answer on the criminal law exam, but that you can answer any three of the questions on the land law paper.

You must make sure that you know where the exam venue is; in fact, if necessary, make a visit to the venue before the date of the exam if you are unsure. You should also ensure that you have your travel arrangements firmly sorted in advance of the date, and that you arrive at the exam venue in good time; remember, it is better to arrive an hour early rather than 2 minutes before the start or, worse, late.

Consider making a checklist for each exam you are sitting that you can consult on the morning of the exam, to ensure that you have everything you need before you leave home. Such a checklist might include:

- a note of the time, date and venue of the exam;
- the time of any buses or trains that you are relying on for transport;

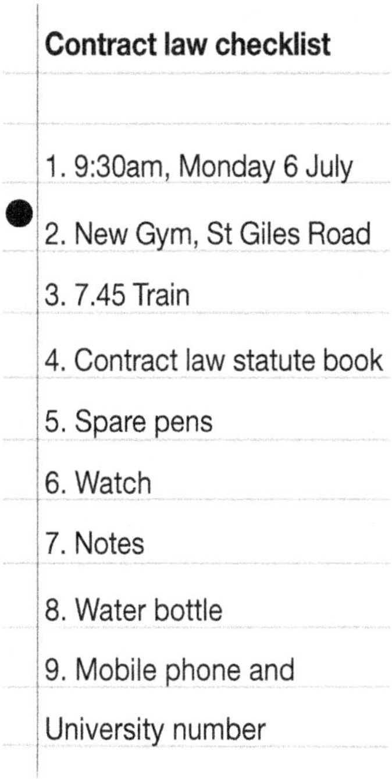

Contract law checklist

1. 9:30am, Monday 6 July

2. New Gym, St Giles Road

3. 7.45 Train

4. Contract law statute book

5. Spare pens

6. Watch

7. Notes

8. Water bottle

9. Mobile phone and

University number

Figure 7.1 Example checklist

- any permitted materials (e.g. a statute book);
- spare pens;
- a watch;
- a drink (to ensure you do not become dehydrated in the exam);
- your mobile phone;
- your institution's phone number in case of emergency;
- your notes.

7.4.2 Preparing for the exam

7.4.2.1 Attending classes

One of the best things that you can do to prepare for any of your exams is to attend, and fully engage with, all classes for that module. Doing this will mean that you begin your revision with the best understanding of the topics that are likely to be covered in the exam.

Indeed, your lecturers may even drop hints about the types of thing that may be asked in the exam or spend quite a bit of time explaining a difficult area of law that you may be asked about. In addition, your tutors may provide guidance about how to answer certain types of question. If they do, follow their advice.

LECTURERS' THOUGHTS	
Heather	'If students have been given guidance before an exam I can't understand why they don't follow it rather than adopt their own approach.'

Also, if your lecturer puts on a revision class prior to the exam, make certain that you attend.

LECTURERS' THOUGHTS	
Heather	'I often put on revision sessions for students in the lead up to the exam and I find that many of them don't attend. It's very foolish on their part.'

It is a relatively common phenomenon whereby students who fail to maintain their attendance at classes can survive reasonably well until exam time, when their lack of engagement with the module is made crashingly apparent by their inability to recognise even the basics the questions are asking about.

7.4.2.2 Question spotting

There is every possibility that you will have a good idea about what topics will be covered in the exam questions. This might be because the lecturer has dropped a number of hints throughout the module, because of the amount of class time you have spent examining a particular matter, or for some other reason.

Such information can be useful in helping you focus your revision. However, you should exercise some caution. Ask yourself how solid your evidence is that you will be asked a particular question.

Also, even if your evidence that a particular topic will be asked about is fairly solid, make sure that you have a back-up, an alternative, just in case the question you are anticipating does not appear on the exam, or if it turns out to be one you would find difficult to answer.

7.4.2.3 Active revision

It should go without saying that your revision should be something in which you engage in the weeks leading up to the exam, rather than something you do just the day, or night, before.

It also goes without saying that your revision should entail you reading your lecture and seminar notes, as well as the relevant parts of any textbooks. However, it should be more than this: your revision should be such that it keeps you actively engaged with the material throughout. To achieve this, your reading should be interspersed with other activities, with the aim of keeping you as immersed in the material as possible.

One of the most useful activities you can do when revising is frequently to test your knowledge. You can do this in a variety of ways, including:

- using multiple-choice questions;
- making use of the seminar questions you have been given throughout the module;
- attempting questions from past exam papers;

- writing your own questions to test yourself on legal authority;
- working with your fellow students to test your knowledge.

Undertaking such activities will achieve a number of things. It will help give focus to your revision and help you engage with the material better than you would if you were simply passively reading. It will also help to highlight any gaps in your knowledge or understanding. Finally, testing yourself in this way will help your memory.

PAST PAPERS

I strongly advise you to try to obtain some past exam papers for the module you are taking and to practise answering the questions within them. This will do a number of things:

- Like the other tests I mention below, it will help you identify areas where your knowledge or understanding is not as strong as you would like.
- It will help give you an indication of the types of question that are asked in the exam (though you should be cautious here – the questions on the past papers may not reflect the content of the exam you are sitting).
- You can, and should, use them to practise writing answers in exam conditions, which will help you to gauge how much you can write in the time allowed and, consequently, better manage your time in the exam.

When practising with past exam papers, you might also find it helpful to make use of question and answer (Q & A) books. These give sample answers to exam questions. They can be beneficial in giving you ideas about how to structure answers to different types of question and about the appropriate level your answers should be at.

You should, though, be careful not to over-rely on Q & A books. Remember, these are general texts, and the questions asked in your exam may be wholly different and so require different answers to those in such books.

MULTIPLE-CHOICE QUESTIONS

Multiple-choice questions are a great way to test and reinforce your knowledge and to make clear where it could be improved.

Many textbooks have multiple-choice questions on their companion websites that you can use. You can sometimes access these even if you haven't purchased the book. You may be able to find them, and perhaps other web-based tests, by using an Internet search engine to look for, say, 'tort multiple-choice questions' (though make sure they are questions from your jurisdiction).

TIP BOX

You may be able to find freely available multiple-choice questions on the internet by, say, typing 'Tort Multiple Choice Questions' into an Internet search engine (though, ensure that the questions are for your jurisdiction).

LEGAL AUTHORITY QUESTIONS

You can write your own questions to test, and help you remember, case law and statutory legal authority.

Index cards or paper squares would be ideal for this. You can write the name of a relevant case on one side of the card and the legal proposition for which it is authority on the other. See Figure 7.2, for example. As is probably obvious, you can read the case name to test whether you can remember the legal proposition, or vice versa.

Entick v Carrington

The 1765 case in which
Lord Camden CJ adhered to
the principle that the
Government must act
lawfully

Figure 7.2 Card with legal proposition and relevant case

You can adopt the same method to help you remember case facts or important statutory provisions; see Figures 7.3 and 7.4, for example.

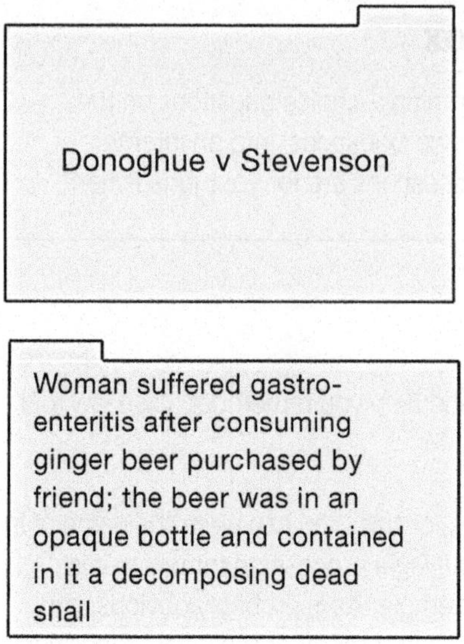

Donoghue v Stevenson

Woman suffered gastro-enteritis after consuming ginger beer purchased by friend; the beer was in an opaque bottle and contained in it a decomposing dead snail

Figure 7.3 Card with case facts

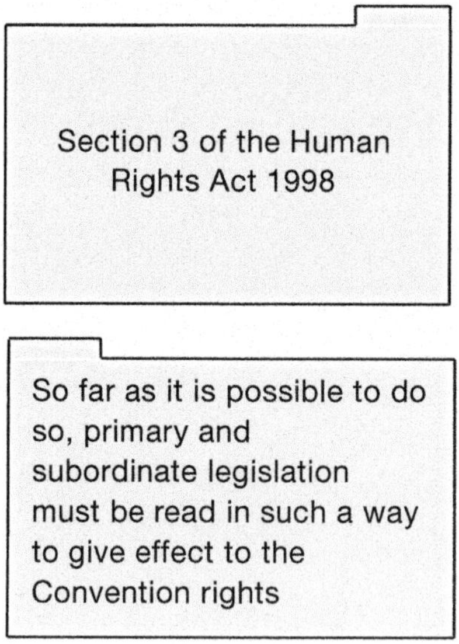

Section 3 of the Human Rights Act 1998

So far as it is possible to do so, primary and subordinate legislation must be read in such a way to give effect to the Convention rights

Figure 7.4 Card with statutory provisions

SEMINAR QUESTIONS

It is likely that, throughout your module, you have been asked to prepare answers to questions so that they can be discussed in seminars or other classes.

These questions can be a valuable self-test resource when it comes to revising, not least because they indicate the subject areas that your lecturers think are important and that you may, therefore, be asked about on the exam.

WORKING WITH OTHERS

Working with your fellow students can be a valuable way to revise and for you to help each other. You can meet with others to discuss ideas or to test one another. However, if you do work with others, you need to be careful of a couple of things.

- First, make sure that you use your time with your fellow students constructively, to revise. Do not use it simply as an excuse to do some extra socialising.
- Second, be careful of the dangers of group-think whereby you convince yourself that something must be correct through a combination of wishful thinking and a mistaken belief in safety in numbers (that you can't all be wrong, or, if you are all wrong, it is better than being wrong on your own). Such group-think may lead you to make mistaken assumptions about what is on the exam ('there won't be a question on defamation'). It may also lead you collectively to misunderstand an area of law.

In brief, working with friends may be productive, but you should be careful that you do not allow yourself to be led into error.

7.4.2.4 Revision planning

You should give thought to planning when you are going to revise and you might find it useful to produce a revision timetable. If you do, you should bear the following principles in mind:

1   Do not spend an inordinate amount of time producing a fancy-looking timetable simply to escape from, and to the detriment of, engaging in proper revision.
2   The first dates you should enter on your timetable are those of the exams you are taking.
3   Be honest with yourself about when and how you work best and construct your timetable around that. For instance, it might be that you work best by

reading in the morning and testing yourself later in the day. It might work better for you dealing with one subject one day and a different one the next; alternatively, you might be better spending half a day on, say, tort law, followed by half a day on criminal law.

4   Make sure you build some breaks into your timetable (which might simply be half an hour doing something different, such as a household chore).

5   Make sure that you take account of any other commitments (work, family, etc.) that you might have.

6   Ensure that you get plenty of sleep.

7   Make such that your planning is flexible to accommodate change (for instance, if you decide that a different way of working might be better) or unforeseen circumstances.

8   Be prepared to change your approach if it becomes apparent that something is not working for you. Remember, an exam timetable is made for you and not vice versa.

<table>
<tr><td colspan="2" align="center">**LECTURERS' THOUGHTS**</td></tr>
<tr><td>**Graham**</td><td>'[I advise students] when producing a revision timetable, be realistic, set realistic goals. If you don't, you'll find yourself tweaking your timetable rather than revising.'</td></tr>
</table>

7.4.3   The day of the exam

Do your best to ensure you get a good night's sleep before the exam.

Before you leave the house, make sure that you have everything that you need (see Section 7.4.1 above). You should plan to get to the exam early and, to this end, make sure that your travel plans are settled beforehand.

It is usually best not to revise just before the exam, as this might increase your nerves. It will be useful, though, to have your notes with you just in case you need to check something at the last minute.

Finally, you should try to avoid people or situations that are likely to make you feel more nervous or less confident.

7.4.4   In the exam

In the examination room, before the exam begins, make sure that you listen to any instructions given by the invigilators and that you carefully read the exam instructions, so that you are clear about what is required. In particular, make certain that you know:

* how many questions you need to answer;
* whether there are any compulsory questions or elements;
* what the weighting of each question is (i.e. how many marks, or what percentage of the overall marks, is each question worth);
* what the finish time of the exam is.

If you are not sure about any of the above, ask one of the invigilators before the exam starts.

If there is any reading time, use it to decide which questions you are going to answer. If you are permitted to make notes during the reading time, start making a plan for the answer to your first question.

SPEND THE CORRECT AMOUNT OF TIME ON EACH ANSWER

LECTURERS' THOUGHTS	
Graham	'The other obvious issue with exams is poor time management, [for instance, students] not devoting equal time to three questions that have equal marks.'

When the exam begins, make sure that you spend the time on each question that is warranted by its weighting. So, for instance, if you have a two-hour exam in which you have to answer three questions of equal weighting (i.e. worth an equal percentage of the overall mark), then you should spend 40 minutes – no more and no less – on each. Do not be tempted to spend more time on one question at the expense of the others; the extra marks you achieve by spending more time on one question will probably not be offset by those you lose on the questions you spent less time on.

COMMON ERROR

Do not spend more time on one question at the expense of the others. The extra marks you earn by spending more time on one will probably not compensate for those you lose by spending less time on another.

ANSWER THE QUESTION

You must remember to answer the questions asked. As with coursework, one of the most common errors students make in exams is that they fail to answer the question; instead, they write all that they know about, say, offer and acceptance.

COMMON ERROR

Rather than answering the question asked, students in exams often write all that they know about a particular subject.

To avoid this dumper-truck approach (see Section 6.3 of Chapter 6), think about what the question is asking you in particular (and you might want to consult Chapter 5 now for some advice about understanding essay and problem questions).

PLAN YOUR ANSWER

You should make a plan for each answer. This will give your answer some structure and, additionally, may help make certain that you are answering the question. In Chapter 6, Section 6.4.2 gives advice about planning an answer to a coursework question, and you should use a (very much abbreviated) adaptation of that method, or something similar, when planning your exam answers.

ANSWER STRUCTURE

Your answers for exam questions should have the same structure as for coursework questions:

- an introduction
- the main part
- a conclusion.

However, your introduction and conclusion should be a lot more basic in answers to exam questions than to coursework questions, and you should not waste precious time repeating the information that forms the main part of your answer.

MAKING CORRECTIONS

As noted above, one of the primary differences between coursework and exams is that markers will be a little more forgiving of mistakes in the latter than in the former. Indeed, though you should not overdo it, it is perfectly acceptable to make amendments to exam answers, such as crossing out and the like.

Similarly, if you forget to mention something, it is permissible to add it later, perhaps at the end of your work, and to direct your marker to the place where it should have been by use of, say, a numbered asterisk, as in Figure 7.5.

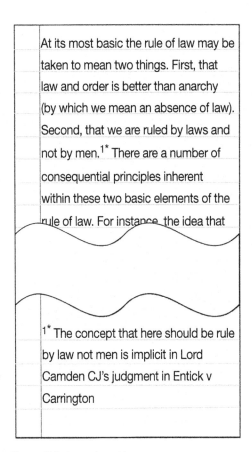

At its most basic the rule of law may be taken to mean two things. First, that law and order is better than anarchy (by which we mean an absence of law). Second, that we are ruled by laws and not by men.[1*] There are a number of consequential principles inherent within these two basic elements of the rule of law. For instance the idea that

[1*] The concept that here should be rule by law not men is implicit in Lord Camden CJ's judgment in Entick v Carrington

Figure 7.5 Amendment to exam answer

To facilitate such amendments, your writing should be neatly spaced, so that the words are not too cramped together, and you should leave a line gap between each paragraph and a blank page after each answer.

Although your marker will be forgiving of some presentational errors, you should do all that you can to make your work legible. Remember, your marker cannot mark your work if they cannot read it.

TIP BOX

Your writing in exams must be legible. Remember, your marker cannot give you marks if they cannot read your work.

LENGTH OF ANSWERS

As a marker of exams, I encounter (far too often) answers – on which I expected students to spend, say, 45 minutes – that are merely a paragraph or half a page long. I often wonder what mark students expect for such work.

I suspect that the student's motivation for such short answers is to leave the exam as early as possible. This is the cardinal error when sitting exams. Never leave early. First, if you have taken the advice given earlier in this chapter about using past exam papers to help you manage your time in exams (Section 7.4.2.3), then you should not be in a situation where you have answered your questions in less time (and, consequently, produced less of an answer). Moreover, there is always proofreading and correcting that can be done.

It may be that, during the exam, all your friends are sitting in the sunshine, drinking beer and having a fine time, and that you would dearly wish to join them. However, the results from the exam might have an effect on your overall degree classification, or may sully an otherwise exemplary academic transcript, and, for that reason, you should stay to the end and use your time to try to get the best mark you can.

IF YOU RUN OUT OF TIME

If you have followed the advice so far in this chapter, it is to be hoped that you will never be in a position where you are running out of time. However, if you are in this position, write in bullet points and try to get as much substance down as possible, addressing as much of the question as you can in the time permitted.

> ## COMMON ERROR
>
> It is a common error (that you should avoid) for students to leave exams early and, consequently, not give as full, or as good, an answer as they otherwise might do.

7.5   DEALING WITH NERVES

It is common to be nervous before and during exams; indeed, some nervousness may even be useful to keep you alert and attentive. Yet, for some students, exam nerves can be a real impediment to their achieving their full potential.

Universities and other higher-education institutions often put on classes for students around exam periods, giving practical advice about dealing with nerves. If exam nerves have a disproportionate effect on you, and such classes are available, you should attend them.

If you are overcome with nerves during an exam, take a short break of a few minutes, close your eyes and breathe slowly, holding each breath for a couple of seconds. This should help you to calm down.

If your mind goes blank, just make rough notes of anything that you can remember about the subject matter of the question and see if you can start making relevant links to form an answer. If that does not work, and it is possible for you to do so, try to answer a different question and come back to the one with which you are struggling – the break away from the troublesome question might allow your mind the time to access the relevant information (a little like when you forget something until an hour or so later, when your brain suddenly produces what was previously lost).

If all else fails, you should simply write the best answer that you can (even if it involves you taking the dumper-truck approach and not really answering the question). Doing this might mean that you write enough to obtain a pass mark for that question, or, if not, that in combination with the marks for your other answers, you write enough substance to get you an overall pass mark (and maybe more) for the exam.

7.6   AFTER THE EXAM

You should take some time to relax after the exam, if possible. You might even want to spend some time with your fellow students immediately following the exam. It can sometimes be healthy and cathartic to do this – to talk over the exam, have a kind of debrief and have a good moan about how awful it was (and about how evil your lecturer is for inflicting such things on you).

Be careful, though, not to engage in this too much, so that you start to worry about what you have, or have not, written. There will always be someone willing to tell you (often not correctly) what you should have mentioned and to start you worrying about what cannot be changed. Avoid such people, and such autopsies. They will not do you any good and may even prevent you preparing as well as you can for your next exam.

Chapter 8

Presentations, moots and assessed seminars

In this chapter we will look at:

- what markers are looking for when marking presentations, moots and assessed seminars;
- how you can best prepare for presentations, moots and assessed seminars;
- how to structure your presentation;
- how to prepare for questions that you may be asked in presentations and moots;
- how to make use of presentation software and other visual aids;
- how to make use of, and refer to, legal authority and quotations;
- how to practise and deliver your presentation;
- the etiquette of mooting;
- how to get the best out of assessed seminars.

8.1 PRESENTATIONS

It is very likely that you will be required to undertake a presentation as part of your degree at some point. This may be as part of the assessment of a module you are taking or it may be an unassessed presentation to your fellow students, say in a seminar class.

There are a number of reasons why you may be asked to present, including the following:

- First, public speaking is often seen as one of the central roles of lawyers, at least in the popular imagination, and so it is considered appropriate that it should form part of your degree.

- Second, even for those who do not wish to practise law, giving presentations is an inherent part of many professional jobs, whether one is expected to present to colleagues or customers.
- Third, you may be asked to undertake a presentation as part of a job interview process.
- Fourth, presenting tests your abilities in a different way from written work (and not simply in the obvious way that you are required to speak rather than write). A presentation will test your understanding of the material because being able to explain things, orally, is an indication of your level of understanding. Also, you are likely to be asked questions at the end of your presentation, which may tease out the depth of your understanding. Indeed, such questions will also test your ability to think on your feet.

Presentations are often a source of dread. In fact, a dislike – and, sometimes, a fear – of public speaking is common in most people.

The following sections will help you get the most from presentations. They will give you advice about effectively preparing for presentations – including about writing and practising them – and about how to present to achieve good marks.

8.1.1   What you should find out

To help you effectively prepare for a presentation, there are a number of things that you should try to find out, if necessary by asking your lecturer. As ever, do not rely on your fellow students for this information: find out from official sources.

Finding out the following information beforehand will help you to prepare:

- the date and time of when you are required to make a presentation;
- the venue;
- how long you are expected to present for;
- whether you will be asked questions at the end of your presentation;
- who the audience are – whether there will simply be your lecturers in the room, or others will be present;
- if it is assessed, what the assessment criteria are;
- whether it will be recorded, either in an audio or video recording; assessed presentations are often recorded so that the recording may be sent to the external examiner for them to confirm the marks awarded by the markers;
- whether you are permitted, or even expected, to use visual aids such as presentation software (PowerPoint, Prezi, Keynote); if so, whether you are

expected to bring this with you on the day – say, on a USB memory device – or to email it to one of the lecturers beforehand; also, it is worth you asking what facilities there will be to enable you to operate the software (to click from one slide to the next): whether there will be a remote device or you will have to use a mouse or keyboard attached to the computer;

- whether there is an expectation about how you should dress, e.g. whether you should wear a shirt and tie, a trouser suit, etc.;
- whether there is an expectation that you should sit or stand (standing is generally best for the impression it creates, but, if you have a choice, you should do what you find comfortable).

If possible, you should visit the venue before you are due to present, so that you can see the size of the room and get an idea about where you will be placed and where your audience will be. Among other things, this will give you a sense of how loudly you need to speak.

Box 8.1 YOUR AUTHOR'S EXPERIENCE

I once gave a presentation as part of the interview process for a job. When preparing, I imagined that I would be speaking in a relatively large room, with the audience a few metres in front of me, and so, when practising, I adopted a suitably loud, declamatory voice. As it turned out, on the day, the room was very small, and my audience were within touching distance. Unfortunately, at least at the start of the presentation, my voice remained as loud as it was during my practice. Despite this, I did receive an offer of employment.

8.1.2   What markers are looking for

It is very likely that your lecturers will mark your presentation against pre-established criteria. You should attempt to find out what these criteria are.

Whatever the particulars of the assessment criteria, generally speaking, your lecturers will:

- be forgiving and understanding of any nerves that you have when presenting;
- make an assessment about the content of your presentation, in particular, about whether it answers the question;

- evaluate how well it is delivered in terms of:
    - whether it is delivered in a monotone voice or whether you speak with enthusiasm and evident interest so as to engage your audience;
    - whether it is simply read or you make eye contact with your audience;
    - the pace of your delivery – whether it is too fast or too slow;
- how well you are able to respond to questions.

8.1.3 Preparing your presentation

8.1.3.1 Choosing your presentation topic

Usually, when asked to do a presentation as an undergraduate student, you are presenting in answer to a question provided by your lecturer.

If, however, you are asked to choose your own topic – and title – on which to present, you may find the advice given in Section 9.5 of Chapter 9 useful. In addition, bear the following principles in mind:

- It is sometimes helpful to frame the title of your presentation as a question, which you then answer.
- You will engage more with the material, and may give a more enthusiastic and engaging delivery, if you choose something in which you are interested.
- Do not make the subject matter of your presentation so wide that what you actually say has no depth; for example, discussing the development of defences to murder from 1700 to the present day in a 10-minute presentation will mean that you say very little of substance.

8.1.3.2 Length

The length of time you need to speak for will be specified by your lecturer. When calculating how much you need to write to fill that time, remember that, generally speaking, you should speak more slowly when presenting than you do in normal speech (though I suppose this depends on how slowly you normally speak).

An appropriate talking speed when presenting is between 110 and 120 words per minute (WPM), and knowing your talking rate can help guide you in how much you need to write. You might want to calculate your own presentation talking rate; to do this:

- Find an electronic version of a document (e.g. one of your pieces of coursework) where the word-programming software is able to tell you the word count.
- Read from it out loud, at a nice, slow pace that you would be comfortable presenting at.
- Time yourself reading for a minute and use the program to tell you how much you have read (you can usually do this by highlighting the text you have read, and the program will tell you how many words are in the highlighted section).
- The number of words read is your WPM talking time.

The length of your presentation – in words – is simply your WPM multiplied by the length of time for which you have been allocated to speak. So, if your presentation talking speed is 110 WPM and you have to present for 10 minutes, then your presentation should have a word length of no more than 1,100 words.

It is likely that, when you come to deliver your presentation, your talking speed will increase because of nerves. This is not necessarily a problem, because you probably would not want to go right to the last second of your allotted time or, worse, go over. In fact, if you exceed your allotted time, you may have your mark reduced, or your markers may simply stop you before you have finished.

However, you should not be significantly below your allotted time (for instance, speaking for only 7 minutes rather than 10), as this will most likely lose you marks.

8.1.3.3   The structure of your presentation

When planning your presentation (i.e. what you are going to say), you might want to read the advice given in Section 6.4.2 of Chapter 6, which is applicable here.

Also, as with coursework, your presentation should have three parts: an introduction, the main part, and a conclusion.

INTRODUCTION

The introduction should spell out to your listeners, in broad terms, what they are going to hear: that is, the basic structure of your presentation. For an example, see Figure 8.1.

In answering the question of the difference
between Hart and Dworkin with regard to hard
cases, I will examine three things. First, how such
cases demonstrate that … Second, how Hart's rule
of recognition … And, finally, why Dworkin rejects
the idea that …

Figure 8.1 Example introduction

THE MAIN PART

The main part of your presentation does the majority of the work to answer the
presentation question. Its content depends, obviously, on the question set by your
lecturers and your answer. There are, though, some general principles that might
be useful to guide you.

First, your presentation needs to be made up of clear messages, clearly
articulated. Remember, unlike with a piece of coursework, your listener cannot re-
read a passage to try to ascertain its meaning if it is not immediately apparent. You
should, therefore, make the effort to convey your arguments as plainly and simply
as possible. There is a balance to be struck here between, on the one hand, having
your presentation so over-complicated and dense that your listener will struggle to
make sense of it and, on the other, its being so simplistic that it lacks substance.

Second, your presentation should logically progress from one point to the next.
Remember, your audience needs to follow your argument, and so you need to
adequately signpost (i.e. ensure that they know where you are taking them in your
argument) and, if necessary (particularly for more complex presentations),
occasionally remind them what you have said, without being repetitive.

THE CONCLUSION

The conclusion should draw together the main strands of your argument in a way
that answers the presentation question.

8.1.3.4 To write out fully or not

Whenever I present, I write out in full exactly what I intend to say. I have this text
with me when I deliver (more as a security blanket, because, in practice, I rarely

look at it). My text is liberally interspersed with big, bold subheadings that act as my cues – my prompts – when I deliver. It looks something like Figure 8.2.

You will notice that I also have anything that I might need to read precisely (such as a legislative provision), or that I don't want to forget to say, in bold, so that I can easily see it.

When I do deliver the presentation, I do not read it and do not stick precisely to it. However, having it written in full facilitates my practising and, when I do practise, helps me get my phrasing just right.

Many would advise you not to take this approach, because it may tempt you into the sin of reading. The alternative that is often suggested is to have the main points of your presentation on, say, cue cards and to use these as your framework, which you fill with detail from memory.

NO GROUNDS NEEDED

In the first place, it is a reasonably well settled law that a uniformed officer does not need any grounds to stop a vehicle provided she does not act capriciously or in bad faith (**section 163 of the Road Traffic Act 1988**).

So the random stopping of this car was lawful.

LICENCE, MOT, INSURANCE

Once stopped, a driver may be asked to provide their driving documents: driving licence; MOT certificate and certificate of insurance. If they can't do so immediately, they are permitted **seven days** to produce them at a police station specified by them – the driver.

HOWEVER – REAS GROUNDS

However, if a constable has reasonable grounds for believing that the vehicle is being driven without a licence or insurance, he may seize the vehicle. The police are given this power under **section 165A of the Road Traffic Act 1988**.

Figure 8.2 Subheadings in full text

NO GROUNDS NEEDED s. 163 of the Road Traffic Act 1988	LICENCE, MOT, INSURANCE 7 DAYS	SEIZE WITH REAS GROUNDS section 165A of the Road Traffic Act 1988
1	2	3

Figure 8.3 Example cue cards

Not only will this prevent you from simply reading your presentation, it will also (it is hoped) lead to a more naturalistic, conversational delivery (which is good).

TIP BOX

If you use cue cards, you should number them so that, if you drop them, you can quickly put them back in order.

You, of course, need to decide which of the above approaches works best for you. It may be that you write your presentation in full in order to practise, but that, when you deliver, you use cue cards (though you should not use cue cards for the first time when you actually present but should practise with them beforehand).

8.1.3.5 Preparing for questions

It is almost certain that you will be expected to answer questions after the delivery of your presentation. In fact, if the presentation is assessed, the competency with which you respond to questions is likely to be part of the assessment (and, hence, will contribute to the mark you receive). I write about answering questions in Section 8.1.7.4, below. Here, I offer advice about how you can prepare for such questions.

In broad terms, post-presentation questions can be divided into two types:

- questions that are asked in response to something in your presentation;
- questions that are asked to everyone presenting on the same topic.

The second of these will be common where students are being assessed, because the markers will want to ensure equality of treatment by asking all those presenting the same, or virtually the same, questions.

It is unlikely that you will know the questions that will be asked in advance, which makes it difficult to prepare for this part of the assessment. The best advice I can give is that you should try to think of all the possible questions that you could be asked – about the subject matter of your presentation in general or your presentation in particular – and draft possible answers. Doing this will provide you with a network of answers to possible questions, which will mean that – even if you are asked a question that you had not anticipated – you may well have thought of a similar question and appropriate answer that you can adapt. This will also help you to develop a thorough understanding of the subject matter of your presentation, which will itself mean that you are better able to deal with any questions that you are asked.

LECTURERS' PET HATES

'One of my pet hates in oral presentations or in moots is when students struggle to move away from their script to deal with questions. Students struggle if they don't thoroughly know their argument.'

8.1.4   Presentation software and other visual aids

Your presentation may be enhanced if it is supported by visual aids such as PowerPoint (or similar presentational software), use of an overhead projector (OHP) or visualiser, or handouts. Indeed, the use of some kind of visual aid may be positively expected.

Among other things, visual aids can help the audience appreciate the structure of your presentation and, in turn, better understand it. In fact, you can use them for some initial signposting to accompany your introduction (to inform your audience of the main strands of your presentation), as well as providing a summary of your argument when concluding.

You can also use visual aids to provide factual information such as case names (and their citation), legislative provisions and quotations.

Whichever type of visual aid you use, you must make sure that the way it looks and the way in which you use it are as professional as possible.

8.1.4.1 Presentation software

There is an increasing amount of presentation software available. The best known, and possibly most used, is Microsoft's PowerPoint. Perhaps the next two most popular are Prezi and Apple's Keynote.

It is beyond the remit of this book to instruct you in the use of this software. The institution at which you are studying may provide training in its use. In any case, this type of software is very user friendly and often has help or instruction features built in.

The following principles may help guide you in the use of such software:

- Presentation software should be used to complement your spoken presentation, not to do the work for you by replacing parts of it.
- A good use of such software is to signpost: to inform your audience of the general structure of your presentation and to inform them – by use of a subheading, for example – of when you move on to a new strand of your argument.
- You should make certain that any text or diagrams that you display are sufficiently large, so that your audience can easily see them.
- You can use presentation software to provide case names (and their citations), legislative provisions and fully referenced quotations (though you should take care not to overuse quotations: your lecturers are interested in your thoughts, not other people's simply stitched together by you).
- Never provide your audience with the full text of your spoken presentation – doing so will mean that they half-listen to you and half-read the text and do not give either their full attention.

66 99	**LECTURERS' THOUGHTS**
Heather	'If they use PowerPoint, do not put [on the slides] everything they wish to say. It should just have the main points [and] act as an aide memoire.'

- Do not use too many slides – you should not be constantly displaying new information to your audience, because this may detract from your overall message.

COMMON ERROR

If you use too many slides they will distract rather than engage your audience.

- Use enough colours and features to make your slides interesting, but not so many that they detract from you and what you are conveying.
- When presenting, face the audience, not the screen (so that they can clearly hear you); do not stand in front of the screen.

WORK SMARTER

Use presentation software to provide your audience with the basic structure of your presentation, to inform them of when you move on to a new theme, and to keep them abreast of which point you are currently addressing.

SLIDES YOU SHOULD INCLUDE

If you are using PowerPoint or similar software, I suggest that your presentation should have, as a minimum, slides that perform the following tasks, in addition to any others you may use:

- a title slide giving the title of your presentation and your name – see Figure 8.4;
- an outline slide to be displayed during the introduction of your presentation, to inform the audience of its basic structure – see Figure 8.5;
- a summary slide summarising the main points of your presentation, which should be displayed during the conclusion – see Figure 8.6;
- An 'Any questions?' slide at the end of your presentation. This will also inform your audience that you have finished.

8.1.4.2 Overhead projectors and visualisers

The prevalence of PowerPoint and similar software has meant that OHPs and visualisers are now infrequently used.

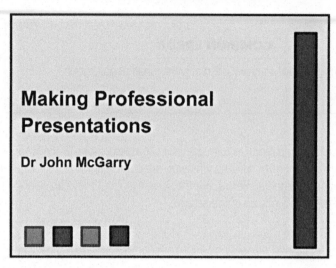

Figure 8.4 Example title slide

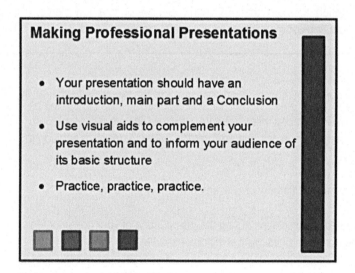

Figure 8.5 Example outline slide

Most readers will be familiar with OHPs. These use transparent slides on which is printed (or sometimes handwritten) text or diagrams, which are then projected on to a screen for the audience to see. Visualisers perform virtually the same task, but they do not need transparencies: they can project from normal (i.e. opaque) pages.

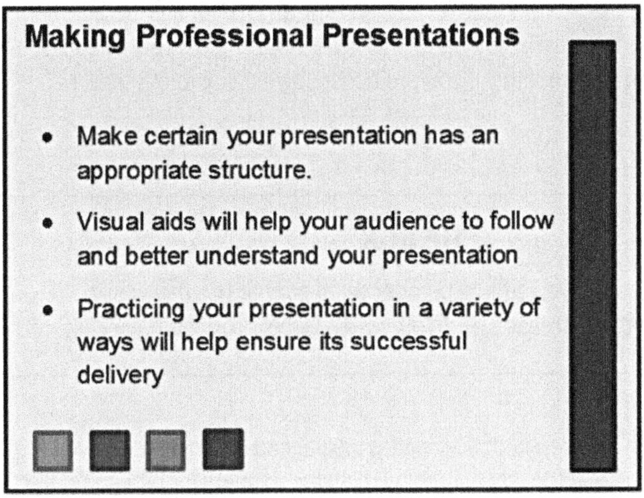

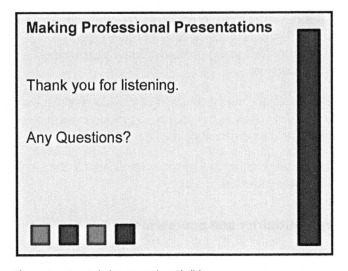

Figure 8.6 Example summary slide

Figure 8.7 Example 'Any questions?' slide

Many of the principles provided in the previous section, with regard to presentation software, apply – with the necessary changes – to OHPs and visualisers. In particular, you should make sure that any text or diagrams are sufficiently large and clear so that your audience can easily see them.

You should, though, use fewer slides if you are using an OHP or a visualiser than you would if using presentation software. This is because the delivery of your presentation will not run smoothly if you are constantly having to physically change the slides.

TIP BOX

If you are using slides, you should number them so that you can easily arrange them in the correct order if you, for instance, drop them.

Finally, make certain that you print your slides well ahead of time, so that you are not attempting to do so at the last minute, with all the dangers (of broken printers and the like) that might entail and the consequent effect on your nerves.

8.1.4.3   Handouts

Like the other visual aids mentioned above, handouts can be used to complement your spoken presentation. They can provide the broad structure of your presentation to your audience. You can also use them to provide case names, legislative provisions and quotations.

As with OHP or visualiser slides, you must make sure that you print handouts well ahead of time. You should also make sure that you have a sufficient number of copies for your audience, printing more than you need if necessary.

I advise you to ask your lecturer whether they think the provision of handouts is necessary to supplement your presentation.

8.1.5   Use of legal authority and quotations

As with any other work you do as a law student, you must provide the authority that substantiates any legal proposition you make in your presentation. This might be case law or statutory authority; it might also be the opinion of an academic (e.g. 'As Hart argues in *The Concept of Law* . . .').

When referring to cases, you should speak the case name; it is not necessary to say the citation – though you should provide this via your visual aids if using them. Moreover, do not give the facts of the case unless this is necessary for the point you are making.

When speaking case names, remember, in UK law, we do not say 'vee' or 'versus'. So, we do not say 'Donoghue vee Stevenson' or 'Donoghue versus Stevenson'. Rather, in civil cases, we say 'and'. So, *Donoghue v Stevenson* is spoken as 'Donoghue *and* Stevenson'.

In criminal cases, we say 'against' instead of 'vee'. We also say the Crown or the Queen instead of 'R'. So, *R v Jones* is pronounced as 'The Crown *against* Jones' or 'The Queen *against* Jones' (or 'The King against Jones', if the case was decided when the monarch was a king).

We also say 'against' in judicial review cases. So, the case *R (Jackson) v Attorney General* would be said as 'The Queen, on behalf of [or 'on the application of'] Jackson against the Attorney General'. Older judicial review cases, written as, say, *R v Secretary of State for the Home Office, ex parte Fire Brigades Union*, would be spoken as 'The Queen against the Secretary of State for the Home Office, *ex parte* the Fire Brigades Union'.

However, when talking of criminal or judicial review cases, it is usually permissible to simply say an abbreviated version of the case name, so that *R v Jones* is simply 'Jones' and *R (Jackson) v Attorney General* is the Jackson case (though you should provide the full case name and its citation in any visual aid).

Table 8.1 How to refer to cases

Case type	Written as	Spoken as
Civil	*Donoghue v Stevenson*	'Donoghue and Stevenson'
Criminal	*R v Jones*	'The Crown against Jones', 'The Queen against Jones' or, simply, 'Jones'
Judicial review	*R (Jackson) v Attorney General*	'The Queen, on behalf of [or 'on the application of'] Jackson against the Attorney General' or 'the Jackson case'.
	R v Secretary of State for the Home Office, ex parte Fire Brigades Union	'The Queen against the Secretary of State for the Home Office, *ex parte* the Fire Brigades Union' or 'The Fire Brigades Union case'

Quotations

It may be appropriate to use quotations to support the arguments you make in your presentation. You should, though, keep their use to a minimum and try to keep them short.

Remember, when you use quotations, you should not alter them from the original without making it clear to your audience that you have done so. There are two ways to do this:

- First, if you introduce something into the quotation because this is necessary in the context in which you use it to make it grammatical or make sense, you should place the additional material in square brackets.
- Second, if you delete any of the quotation – say, because it is not necessary for the point you are making or to make the quotation grammatical in the context in which you use it – you should inform your audience of this using an ellipsis (three dots).

See Section 10.5 in Chapter 10 for some examples of how to do this.

8.1.6   Practising

You *must* practise your presentation before you deliver it – lots of times and in different ways (e.g. on your own, before friends, etc.). You should always practise out loud, rather than silently reading through it. If you intend to use a visual aid to complement your spoken presentation, this should be included in your practising.

The benefits of practising include the following:

- You will get accustomed to the material and to speaking it aloud.
- It will help you to remember your material, which will mean that your delivery is likely to be more natural.
- It will help you gauge your timing and assess whether your presentation is too long or too short. To enable this, you should always time yourself when practising.
- It will help you deal with any anxiety by making the act of presenting more familiar – the more you do it, the easier it will become.
- It will help you remember when to move to the next slide if you are using presentation software, an OHP or a visualiser.

TIP BOX

If, when practising, you find yourself repeatedly stumbling over a particular word or phrase, consider changing it to something you find easier to say.

You should practise delivering your presentation in different situations, such as:

- in front of a mirror;
- in front of friends or family;
- by making an audio or video recording of yourself when presenting.

After each practice, reflect on your delivery and ask yourself, honestly, what could be improved. If you have practised in front of an audience, ask them for some constructive feedback.

8.1.7   Delivering your presentation

8.1.7.1 Nerves

It is natural to feel some nerves when presenting. Even some very experienced presenters get nervous (and you would no doubt be surprised at how many of your lecturers this applied to). Moreover, your audience – and your markers, if your presentation is assessed – will be understanding and forgiving of some nervousness.

You should, though, have some strategies to deal with any nerves you suffer, so that they do not become so debilitating that they prevent you performing as well as you can.

For a start, you should make sure that you have some water to hand when presenting. This will help combat the dry mouth that often accompanies nerves. It will also allow you take a sip and, therefore, to pause from speaking in order to calm yourself.

You might combat your nerves by breathing a little more slowly and deeply than usual both before and during your presentation.

You might also find a visualisation technique to be effective. Try to step into the role of the professional, proficient presenter. That is, rather than thinking of yourself as a student presenting to your lecturers, think of yourself as one professional giving an interesting and informative talk to fellow professionals, who are interested to hear what you have to say.

8.1.7.2 How you should dress

There may be expectations that you should dress in a particular way when presenting, and you should seek clarification on this from your lecturers.

If the presentation is assessed, my advice is that you should dress in the way you would if you were appearing in court (or your nearest approximation). Doing this may help your confidence and help you step into the role of professional presenter. Moreover, even if there are no formal requirements that you should dress in a particular way, your appearance may – consciously or otherwise – help form part of the judgment your audience make about you (and, consequently, the mark you receive).

8.1.7.3 The presentation itself

Before you deliver your presentation, you should turn off your mobile phone, if you have one. You should also conduct a last-minute check that you do not have any (unwanted) undone buttons, unzipped zips, smudged make-up or dinner medals (food stains).

Box 8.2 YOUR AUTHOR'S EXPERIENCE

I once gave a presentation as part of a job interview with – I discovered afterwards but did not know at the time – the zip of my trousers undone (and no doubt visible). I did not receive an offer of employment.

When it comes to the actual presentation:

- Do not simply read from your notes.
- Do not deliver in a monotonous or mumbling voice; rather, you should:
    - clearly articulate; and
    - try to speak in a confident, authoritative and enthusiastic manner.
- It is usually better if you stand rather than sit – you will appear, and feel, more confident and you will better project your voice (if you need to) if you stand.

- Try not to move around too much.
- Face the audience – if not, they may not hear you.
- Try to look members of the audience in the eye; if you find this difficult, look at an imaginary spot in the middle of their forehead.

LECTURERS' PET HATES

'My pet hate with presentations is a lack of engagement [by the presenter], so [for instance] no eye contact.'

If you misspeak, or otherwise make a mistake, do not worry. It has happened to everyone. Simply say what you meant to say and carry on.

TIP BOX

If you don't feel confident, pretend that you do – remember, your audience do not know whether you are confident or not (unless you tell them) so you should 'fake it till you make it'.

8.1.7.4 Answering questions

As noted above, it is very likely that you will be asked questions at the end of your presentation. I gave advice, in Section 8.1.3.5 above, about how you can prepare for such questions.

It is worthwhile keeping in mind that, in most cases, those asking questions are not trying to catch you out. Rather, they are likely to be giving you an opportunity to demonstrate your understanding or to expand on your arguments.

In the presentation itself, when asked questions, you should always pause to think about your answer before replying. If necessary, take a sip of water to buy yourself more time.

LECTURERS' THOUGHTS

Graham	'When asked a question, ensure a pause is taken to digest the question [before answering] – perhaps take a drink of water or clear the throat.'

If you don't properly hear, or understand, ask for the question to be repeated or rephrased; you might even rephrase it yourself to check with the questioner whether you have correctly understood them (which will also buy you more time to think about your answer).

You can, quite legitimately, disagree (respectfully) with your questioner. For instance, you could reply with something like the following: 'I understand your argument, and can see its merit, but I still think that Lord Justice Laws' talk of constitutional statutes in *Thoburn v Sunderland City Council* is a natural extension of the decision in *Factortame*.' Remember, your questioner might not be asking something that reflects their own views; they are most likely giving you a chance to show your understanding of the subject of your presentation.

8.2   MOOTS

A moot is a mock appeal case in which the participants are expected to argue points of law as they pertain to a fictional case that has been appealed from a lower court. Moots are an excellent opportunity for students to practise their advocacy skills.

The mooters will be presented with a fictional scenario (like a problem question), and the points of law that they are expected to argue will be specified. See Box 8.3 for an example.

The mooters should not argue about the facts of the case but should accept them as presented.

The case is heard before a judge or a panel of judges. The judge is primarily there to rule on which team has best presented and argued their case, not to determine its outcome (though, they may do that). The winning team is not necessarily the side that the judge would have decided the case in favour of.

In moots, there are usually two teams of two: leading and junior counsel (advocates) for the appellants (those bringing the appeal) and leading and junior counsel for the respondents (those defending the appeal).

8.2.1   The benefits of mooting

It is almost certain that you will be given the opportunity to moot by your law school. It may even be one of the ways in which you are formally assessed. Your

Box 8.3 IN THE COURT OF APPEAL (CIVIL DIVISION)

R (on behalf of Bull)
– v –
Prime Minister

Following recent difficulties in the European Union between different Member States, the European Council decided that a new EU institution would be created: the European Policy Unit. The role of this institution would be to make policy suggestions to be considered by the European Council concerning the long-term strategic goals of the EU and how these can best be achieved.

The prime minister announced the creation of this body in the House of Commons, stating that it would be brought into being by the signing of a Memorandum of Understanding by the Member States, and that he would sign the Memorandum on behalf of the United Kingdom. In response to a question by John Bull MP, the prime minister stated that there would be no referendum on this matter as the creation of the new body involved no amendment to the EU treaties and its role would be advisory only.

Mr Bull sought a judicial review of the prime minister's decision not to hold a referendum on the grounds that this was contrary to the requirements of the European Union Act 2011. He requested an injunction to prevent the prime minister signing the Memorandum of Understanding.

At first instance, Mardy J held that the creation of the European Policy Unit was not one of the situations listed in the European Union Act 2011 that gave rise to a legal obligation to hold a referendum because: there was no amendment of the EU treaties, and there was no transfer of competence or power. He also held that, in any case, matters of foreign policy are generally not justiciable, and so the court had no power to grant an injunction to prevent the prime minister signing the memorandum.

Mr Bull now appeals to the Court of Appeal on the grounds:

1   The creation of the European Policy Unit satisfied the conditions specified in the European Union Act 2011 so as to require approval by a majority vote in a referendum.
2   That while matters of foreign policy are generally held to be non-justiciable, this is not a universal rule, and the European Union Act 2011 imposes certain legal obligations on the prime minister and the government that the courts have jurisdiction to enforce.

law school may conduct internal mooting competitions (i.e. among students within your law school) or participate in external competitions against other law schools.

If you have the chance to moot, you should take it. This is particularly so if you expect advocacy to be part of your future career, which is likely to be the case for most jobs as legal practitioners, particularly barristers or solicitors (especially solicitors with higher rights of audience: those who have the right to argue cases in all courts). In fact, it is fairly common that those applying for a training contract (with a firm of solicitors) or a pupillage (in barristers' chambers) are asked to confirm in the application that they have mooted while at law school.

Mooting is a great way to develop your public speaking skills, including your confidence about speaking in public and your ability to think on your feet. It is also an excellent way to develop your legal research skills.

8.2.2   Mooting personnel

The moots in which you participate may include some, or all, of the following:

- *The judge*: The judge (or judges) may be one of your lecturers, or they may be a solicitor or barrister from outside the law school; they may even be a practising judge. The judge's role is to rule on matters of procedure and to decide which team has won the moot.
- *Master/mistress of the moots (or mooting master/mistress)*: The master of the moots is often a student. Their role is to organise the moot. This might include: timetabling when moots will take place (especially in a competition), booking a room, arranging a judge and organising the exchange of skeleton arguments and legal authorities.
- *The clerk to court*: The clerk to the court is often a student. They are usually responsible for assisting the judge in court (i.e. in the moot), perhaps by keeping time (to ensure the mooters do not exceed their allotted time) and providing the judge with the relevant legal authorities.
- *The mooters*: There will usually be a leading counsel and junior counsel for the appellants and leading and junior counsel for the respondents.

8.2.3   Order of business

The mooters will be presented with the mooting question some time before the moot. This will usually be a week or so before, though in competition it is not uncommon for the mooters to receive the question on the day of the moot. The two teams will then have the opportunity to research their case and form their arguments.

Often, the teams will be expected to exchange, and provide the court with, their skeleton arguments (the broad summary of their arguments) and a list of the case law authorities on which they intend to rely.

In the moot itself, there are two common approaches governing the order of the speakers (which will be governed by the mooting rules): see Table 8.2.

Though it is not always the case, it is common (as shown in Table 8.2) for the leading counsel for the appellants to have a brief right of reply to the respondent's submission.

Following the conclusion of the submissions, the judge, or judges, will decide which team won, or award marks if the moot is assessed. The judge may also give their opinion on the legal position.

8.2.4 Rules

Each law school, and each competition, will have its own mooting rules with which you should familiarise yourself. This will specify various aspects of how the moot should operate, including:

- the order in which counsel (the mooters) will be called to speak;
- the time permitted for each submission (i.e. the length of time for which each mooter is permitted to speak);

Table 8.2 Order of speakers

Approach 1	Approach 2
Leading counsel for the appellants	Leading counsel for the appellants
Leading counsel for the respondents	Junior counsel for the appellants
Junior counsel for the appellants	Leading counsel for the respondents
Junior counsel for the respondents	Junior counsel for the respondents
Right of reply by leading counsel for the appellants	Right of reply by leading counsel for the appellants

- whether the appellant counsel will have a right of reply;
- whether a skeleton argument has to be exchanged with the other side, and with the courts, and, if so, its maximum length;
- the maximum number of case law authorities that may be relied on.

8.2.5   Addressing the court and other matters of etiquette

A moot is an attempt to recreate the formal atmosphere of an appellate courtroom, and you should behave accordingly. There should be no histrionics or table-thumping. Rather, you should behave in an appropriate, professional and measured manner, dealing with the other participants with courtesy and respect.

You should also adhere to the following:

- Dress smartly, as if appearing in court for real.
- Stand when addressing the court or being addressed by the judge.
- As with presentations, you should speak clearly and more slowly than you normally would when speaking.
- Refer to the judges in the following way (as appropriate): 'My Lord', 'Your Lordship', 'My Lady', 'Your Ladyship'.
- The leading counsel for the appellants, who will be the first mooter invited to speak, is usually expected to introduce him/herself and his/her fellow mooters. For example: 'May it please the court, I, Laura Lawyer, appear for the appellants with my learned friend, Mr Timid [i.e. junior counsel for the appellants]. My learned friends, Miss Nervous and Mr Smartypants, appear for the respondents.'
- The leading counsel for the appellants is usually expected to ask the judge whether he/she would like to be reminded of the facts of the case (i.e. the facts of the mooting problem). This offer will usually be declined, but, if you are lead counsel for the appellants, you should be prepared to give a brief, non-partisan, outline of the facts. For example: 'Would your Ladyship like to be reminded of the facts of this case?'.
- Do not read your submission – you should be sufficiently familiar with your arguments for you to be able to convey them with no, or only occasional, glancing at your notes.
- Address the court (i.e. the judge), not your fellow mooters, and make eye contact with the judge when speaking.
- Do not interrupt the other participants (especially the judge), but be prepared for the judge interrupting you to ask questions.

- Try to keep reasonably still while speaking; try not to gesticulate with your arms or use them for emphasis.
- Say case names in full, along with their citations, e.g. 'The case of Donoghue and Stevenson to be found in the Appeal Cases Law Reports of 1932 at page five hundred and sixty-two'. See Section 8.1.5, above, for advice about speaking case names.
- For each case that you rely on, ask the judge whether he/she wishes to be reminded of the facts; e.g. 'Would your Ladyship like to be reminded of the facts of the case?'. This offer will usually be declined, but you should be prepared for the judge asking to hear the facts simply to test your knowledge.

TIP BOX

Try to attend moots given by other mooters in your law school to get a feel for how the process works and how you should conduct yourself. You might also find it useful to search the internet for videos of moots.

8.2.6   Questions

You should expect to be questioned on your submission by the judge. In fact, the judge may well interrupt you to ask a question; if this happens, you must behave with the utmost politeness and respond to the judge's enquiry; do not show any irritation at being interrupted.

The advice I gave in Section 8.1.3.5, above, may be helpful as you prepare for questions.

Box 8.4 YOUR AUTHOR'S EXPERIENCE

As an undergraduate student, in my first moot, I acted as leading counsel for the appellants. The rules gave me a short right of reply after the respondents had concluded the presentation of their case. However, the judge told me that he'd decided not to permit me this right. As a first-year student, I didn't feel confident enough to disagree and so I meekly accepted this decision. I now suspect, however, that the judge was offering me the opportunity to convince him – politely and respectfully – that the rules meant he could not refuse me the right to a reply.

You should keep in mind that, when asking questions, the judge may not be attempting to catch you out. Rather, he/she is probably giving you an opportunity to demonstrate your skill and understanding.

8.3   ASSESSED SEMINARS

Assessed seminars are becoming more prevalent in law schools as a method of assessing students.

Assessed seminars are similar to unassessed seminars in that you are expected to fully prepare for the class beforehand and to participate in it. The difference is that your participation will be marked, and this mark may form part of the overall mark you receive for that module.

8.3.1   The benefits of assessed seminars

One of the primary benefits of assessed seminars, and one of the reasons why some law schools use them, is that they encourage student attendance, preparation and participation.

This is also a benefit for students who may need such encouragement. In addition, assessed seminars allow you, as a student, to receive marks for work you should do anyway.

8.3.2   Getting the best from assessed seminars

As with any other form of assessment, there will be criteria against which your performance in assessed seminars is marked. You should obtain and familiarise yourself with these criteria so that you know what is required of you to get the best marks.

The assessment criteria will differ from law school to law school. However, it is likely that you will be marked according to the following:

- evidence of the preparation you have undertaken for the class;
- your willingness to contribute to the discussion;
- your ability to listen to and appreciate the views of others – this criterion is usually in place to stop certain students dominating the class and speaking over others;
- your level of understanding.

With regard to the first of these criteria, you should – as a minimum – undertake all the reading asked of you and prepare answers for all the seminar questions. With regard to any cases you have been asked to read, you should be prepared to explain at least the following:

- the facts of the case;
- the decision;
- whether the decision was a unanimous or majority decision, and, if the latter, who the minority judges were and the basis of their dissention;
- why the case is relevant for that class (this is a very important factor when discussing cases in class – you should know why they are relevant).

See Chapter 3 for advice about reading cases.

Ideally, you should be able to talk about the things you have been asked to read with little or no reference to your notes.

LECTURERS' PET HATES

'In seminars, it's so annoying when students aren't able to tell you even the most basic details about a case [that they have been asked to read beforehand] without reading from their notes or, even worse, from a textbook. They should have this stuff at their fingertips, ready to go'

You are, of course, attempting to achieve the best marks you can in assessed seminars and, for this reason, you should volunteer to speak whenever you can, perhaps by raising your hand.

COMMON ERROR

A common error students make in seminars is not to volunteer to speak even when they know the answer. This may be because of shyness and not wanting to speak in front of others. The problem is that remaining silent when they do know the answer leads to a greater chance that the lecturer – who will want them to contribute – may ask them a question for which they do not know the answer.

Assessed seminars are still a learning forum, and so you should ask questions if something is unclear or you do not understand. Indeed, asking intelligent questions may demonstrate the amount of preparation you have undertaken and, also, that you have a good level of understanding.

You should, though, never be in a situation where your lack of understanding is because you have not done the preparation required for the class – I call this the 'I've done no work and I still don't understand' question.

TIP BOX

Try to engage in some reading over and above that which you have been asked to do – for instance, read some relevant journal articles in addition to those you've been asked to read – and, in the class, try to demonstrate to your lecturer that you have done this. For instance, at the relevant point, you could raise your hand and say: 'I read Raz's article 'The Rule of Law and its Virtue' and he seems quite critical of Dicey; in fact he writes: "English writers have been mesmerised by Dicey's unfortunate doctrine for too long"'.

Chapter 9
Dissertations

This chapter will discuss:

- the advantages and disadvantages of doing a dissertation;
- the meaning of legal research;
- what you should attempt to find out before beginning your dissertation;
- how you can identify a suitable research topic;
- what is usually required for a dissertation proposal;
- research methods, methodology and ethics;
- how best to work with your dissertation supervisor;
- the different elements that usually compose a dissertation;
- what is required by a literature review;
- how to choose a dissertation title;
- managing your time.

9.1   INTRODUCTION

It is almost certain that you will be given the opportunity to write a dissertation, usually in the final year of your degree. It might even be that undertaking a dissertation is compulsory, so that you have to do it.

A dissertation is a research project. It is a significant piece of work, much longer than normal coursework. The maximum length of dissertations varies from law school to law school; they will commonly range from 7,000 words in length in some schools to 10,000 words in others.

A dissertation should be an in-depth, critical study of an area of law. Unlike coursework, you will be expected to decide the subject matter and title of your project. There may be some classes giving advice about research in general, research methods and the like, but most of the work will be undertaken independently, by you, outside the classroom. You will be assigned a dissertation supervisor whose role it is to advise you about your project.

9.2 THE ADVANTAGES, AND POTENTIAL DISADVANTAGES, OF DOING A DISSERTATION

Advantages

There are some significant benefits of doing a dissertation in contrast to a taught module.

For a start, you can study and undertake research in an area of law in which you are really interested. Indeed, you might have the opportunity to study something that would not otherwise be available to you in the other modules on your degree. You also have a chance to develop a deep understanding of the subject matter of your dissertation.

Another attraction with dissertations is that, if you do one, it is your own idea and your own work. Students who complete a dissertation often feel a real sense of ownership, of achievement and of pride, much more than they do with any of the other modules they study.

Undertaking a dissertation is also valuable if you intend to take a postgraduate course, particularly if you are considering taking a postgraduate research degree (say, an LLM by Research, an Mphil (master of philosophy) or a PhD (doctor of philosophy)). Indeed, such research degrees are obtained, for the most part, by completing a significant research project, and, so, experience of doing an undergraduate dissertation will be invaluable and will give you a good idea of your aptitude for such work. Likewise, most, if not all, taught masters programmes will require you to undertake a dissertation, and you will find that having completed one as part of your undergraduate degree will be very useful. (See Sections 11.6 and 11.6.1 of Chapter 11 for information about different postgraduate courses.)

Potential disadvantages

Some students find doing a dissertation difficult. Even students who otherwise do well may fail to thrive with a dissertation. There are a number of possible reasons for this.

Some students miss the solid framework offered by taught modules, led by the lecturer, where they turn up for classes at the prescribed time after having undertaken the preparation specified by the lecturer.

Also, students sometimes have difficulties completing a project that they devise themselves. They miss the parameters that are naturally inherent in, say, a coursework question set by the lecturer.

Moreover, many students do not adequately plan their time. Dissertations are usually carried out throughout the final year of an undergraduate degree, the completed article being submitted at the end of the academic year. This means that students doing a dissertation have to devote sufficient time to it during the year, and this can be difficult when there are seemingly more pressing demands on your time, such as coursework that may need to be submitted earlier than your dissertation or exams at the end of the first semester for which you need to prepare. I give advice about managing your time to complete the dissertation in Section 9.10 below.

LECTURERS' THOUGHTS	
Graham	'Students have a lot of freedom when doing a dissertation but they sometimes struggle with this [in terms of time management] as the dissertation work is put off for other things such as coursework.'

9.3   RESEARCH

As mentioned above, a dissertation is a research project. It is often difficult to convey to students what is meant by research in this context.

Research is not simply an opportunity for you to discover something that you did not previously know (but that was known to others). It is not an intellectual meander with an enquiring mind. Nor is it enough to identify some empirical facts (even if they were not previously known), without providing some analysis of them. Furthermore, it is not research simply to give an account of other people's arguments about a particular matter, without any analysis of your own.

So, let's imagine that you discovered that 40 per cent of law firms in London that previously undertook work funded by legal aid had ceased to do so. This, in itself, is not adequate to be classified as legal research. Rather, you would need to use this statistic as the basis, or one of the bases, of your research. For example, you might offer some explanation of the possible or likely cause of this reduction in legal aid work – say, that it is a result of the government's reduction of the legal aid budget. Alternatively (or, perhaps, in addition), you might want to consider the possible implications of what you have found: for instance, you might want to argue that the likely consequence of this reduction is that many in a particular income bracket are effectively denied access to legal advice and representation.

Ideally, then, legal research should involve critical analysis of, and (it is to be hoped) writing something new (and interesting) about, an area of law. 'Area of law' is often broadly defined: as long as you are examining something that has some connection to law or has legal implications, you are likely to be considered to be undertaking legal research.

Some examples of possible legal research projects may help you understand the different types of legal research that may be carried out:

- You might want to examine the implications of a particular legal decision or new legislation, providing analysis of the likely changes it will mean for those it affects; alternatively, you might argue that – despite assumptions to the contrary – the decision or legislation does not alter things very much at all.
- You might want to engage in empirical research. This might involve you obtaining your own data (e.g. through interviews or questionnaires) or making use of data supplied by others (e.g. making use of government statistics). You might then analyse these data to make a particular argument. So, for example, you might interview people who have been stopped by the police while driving and use your responses to consider whether the police are treating such drivers fairly and with courtesy. (Just a note of caution here: if you wish to engage in the type of empirical research where you generate your own data (say, by use of questionnaires, focus groups or interviews), you will most likely need ethical approval from your institution before you begin. Moreover, it may be the case that you are prohibited from engaging in some kinds of empirical research or are strongly advised against doing it. See Section 9.7.4, below, for information and advice about research ethics.)
- You may want to provide a historical analysis of the development of a particular area of law – for instance, you might want to examine, and explain, the development of judicial review in the 1980s.

- It might be that you wish to analyse an area of law from a particular philosophical position: e.g. a feminist critique of employment law.
- A research project might involve a comparative analysis of an area of law – say, looking at the treatment of certain kinds of offender in the UK and another country (or countries); or, how the law deals with anti-competitive practices in the European Union and the United States of America. Some caution needs to be exercised, though, with regard to such comparative research. First, as with all research, you need to be careful that the subject matter of your enquiry is not so broad that you are unable to say anything of substance. Second, you have to ensure that you will be able to access and understand the relevant materials of your comparator country. If you can't access or understand the laws of, say, China – and have little or no understanding of how the Chinese interpret and apply their laws – then you should not choose it as a comparator. Moreover, you should avoid comparative research of this kind that would require you to gather empirical data; at the risk of stating the obvious, you cannot assess how people in the UK feel about the protection of their employment compared with those in Uruguay if you have no access to the latter.
- Often, a critical examination of a particular theory of law is a good research project. Indeed, you might even want to undertake an analysis of one academic's critique of another's theories. So, for instance, it would be possible, and viable, to carry out a critical re-evaluation of H.L.A. Hart's critique of John Austin.

9.4 WHAT YOU SHOULD FIND OUT

If you wish to undertake a dissertation, there are a number of things that you should attempt to discover:

- If you have to provide an initial research proposal, when does this have to be submitted, and what does it need to contain?
- What is the maximum word length of the dissertation, and does this include the bibliography, references and any appendices (i.e. are these included when calculating the word length of your project)?
- Are you permitted to exceed the word limit – for instance, can you exceed it by a certain percentage?
- What is the submission date for the completed dissertation?
- Are there limits to the number of meetings you can have with your supervisor, and are there any particular requirements about when these should take

place (for instance, it might be that your supervisor is prohibited from looking at, and commenting on, any work in the month preceding the submission date).

- Will you need to obtain ethical clearance in order to carry out your research? (See Section 9.7.4 below for information about research ethics.)
- What are the rules governing how the dissertation should be presented? Are there any requirements about:
  - the title page (i.e. what information this should contain, and how it should be formatted);
  - the font – size and type (e.g. at least font size 12 and Times New Roman);
  - whether it must be double-spaced;
  - whether there are any requirements about the page layout, e.g. the size of any margins, where the page numbers should be, how headings and subheadings should be formatted;
  - whether – and, if so, how – it must be bound, and where the binding facilities are?

As ever, you should obtain this information from official sources such as the dissertation module leader or your supervisor, rather than relying on the (often unreliable) opinions of your fellow students.

9.5 CHOOSING A RESEARCH QUESTION

If you do a dissertation, it is likely that you will be expected to frame the subject of your enquiry as a question or questions. This will usually be a main research question, with two or three sub-questions, though it may be two or three equal but interrelated research questions.

Choosing a topic

One of the things that students often find difficult with dissertations is finding suitable subject matter. Let's look first at some general principles you should think about when trying to identify the general subject area in which you might want to research (e.g. public law, contract law, criminal law):

- You have to be interested in the area of law. This might seem like a statement of the blindingly obvious, but it is very important, because you are likely to be

---

Box 9.1 EXAMPLE RESEARCH QUESTIONS

Main research question

What are the implications of the government's cuts to the criminal legal aid budget for those seeking legal advice who would normally qualify for legal aid?

First sub-question

What changes have been made to the criminal legal aid budget since May 2010?

Second sub-question

How have the changes to criminal legal aid changed the provision of legal aid by solicitors in London?

Third sub-question

As a consequence, are those seeking legal advice for criminal cases, who qualify for legal aid, unable to access that advice?

---

working on your dissertation over the course of an academic year, and your commitment to it has to be such to motivate you over that time.

- Be wary about choosing a particular topic because you want to be supervised by a particular member of staff, not least because you may not be assigned that person as your supervisor.
- You should consider whether you want to examine an area that you have previously studied in one of your modules or look at something that is new to you. If the latter, you should note that it might entail a great deal of work to examine an area of law you have not studied, not least because you will have to sufficiently acquaint yourself with the basics before you can even hope to say something worthy of an undergraduate dissertation. Moreover, because you are coming to the subject area with a low level of existing knowledge, it might be difficult for you even to identify a suitable research project.

Once you have determined the general subject area (or areas) in which you are interested, you need to decide what your particular project is going to be; that is, you need to identify your research questions. There are a number of ways you can approach this:

- Ask one of your lecturers who either teaches or researches in that subject area – often, your lecturers might have identified a matter that would make a good research project but that, for one reason or another, they do not want to pursue themselves.
- Look through the relevant journals to see what types of thing have been recently written about. Often, a good research project is one where there has been some recent academic interest, but where you can make a worthwhile contribution. Being 'recent' will mean that it is topical (which is not an essential factor, but it will help sustain your interest and that of your reader). The fact that there is existing academic interest will give you a body of literature on which you can build and may suggest some parameters to your project.
- As ever, keeping abreast of current affairs may help. It may be that there is something in the news that suggests a good research project.
- There are an increasing number of subject blogs on the Internet. For instance, there are well-established blogs in UK constitutional law, UK human rights law, EU law, UK criminal law, etc. A quick glance over such a blog in your general subject area may give you a good idea for a research project. Simply use an Internet search engine to find these blogs.

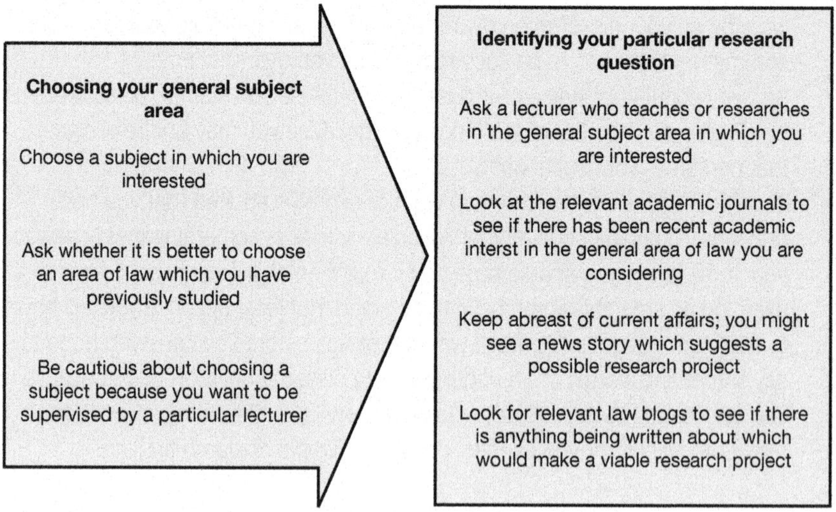

Choosing your general subject area

Choose a subject in which you are interested

Ask whether it is better to choose an area of law which you have previously studied

Be cautious about choosing a subject because you want to be supervised by a particular lecturer

Identifying your particular research question

Ask a lecturer who teaches or researches in the general subject area in which you are interested

Look at the relevant academic journals to see if there has been recent academic interst in the general area of law you are considering

Keep abreast of current affairs; you might see a news story which suggests a possible research project

Look for relevant law blogs to see if there is anything being written about which would make a viable research project

Figure 9.1 Choosing a topic

There are two final principles that you need to remember when framing your research questions. First, keep in mind that it is much better for your research to be narrow and deep rather than so broad that you cannot say anything of substance.

WORK SMARTER

Students often make the mistake, when drafting a research proposal, of trying to cover too much ground. Remember, it is better to examine a narrow area of law in depth rather than a broad area of law which, because of its breadth, means you do not write anything significant.

For example, an 8,000-word research project that attempted to examine the development of the law of defamation in England from 1066 to the present day would be virtually guaranteed to fail, because it could offer no substantial analysis and would struggle to even identify significant milestones. It would be better to narrow the focus, both in terms of time frame and subject matter – to examine, for instance, the development of the so-called Reynolds defence between 1999 (when the defence was first articulated in *Reynolds v Times Newspapers Ltd and Others* [1999] UKHL 45) and the enactment of the Defamation Act 2013.

Second, your project must be doable. This means a number of things:

- The project must be viable in itself (by which I mean, it must be doable in itself).
- It must be such that you have the ability to undertake it in terms of intellectual capacity (and you need to be honest with yourself – you are going to get better marks for a relatively modest project that you successfully complete than for an overly ambitious one with which you struggle).
- You must also have the time and resources to carry it out – in all likelihood, you will not have the money or time to interview people in Northern Ireland, Scotland and Wales to canvass their views about the devolution of power. Likewise (unless you have very good contacts), you are unlikely to gain access to the chief executive officer of BP to ask him about the company's approach to protecting the environment.
- You should also note that there are some projects that your law school may not have the supervisory capacity to adequately supervise.

9.6   RESEARCH PROPOSAL

You may be asked to write a dissertation proposal detailing your planned research project and, possibly, how you intend to undertake it. This might be simply to enable your law school to evaluate whether your proposed project is viable and to assign you a dissertation supervisor.

In some law schools, you may be asked to produce a dissertation proposal that is assessed, and the mark you receive will form part of the final mark for the dissertation module.

Whether the dissertation proposal is assessed or not, you need to ascertain the elements that it should comprise. Table 9.1 gives some of the elements commonly found in a dissertation proposal.

Table 9.1 Elements often contained in dissertation proposals

Element	Description
Title	You should provide a working title that is brief but adequately describes your proposed project
Overview of the proposed research	This should provide the context for your proposed research and give a general account of what it is you intend to do
Research questions	The research questions that your dissertation will seek to answer
Details of your proposed methods and methodology	How you will gather and analyse your research data (the methods) and your overall philosophical approach (the methodology)
Literature review	An account of the existing literature in the area of your proposed research
Proposed structure	How many, and which, chapters you intend your dissertation to be made up of and a brief outline of each one
Timetable	The dates by which you intend to complete different aspects of your dissertation

It is worth noting that your proposal is not set in stone – it is simply an outline of your intended research. It is likely that your project will change as you proceed. Indeed, it is the nature of research that your initial idea will evolve and change. It is sometimes characteristic of less able students that they attempt to rigidly adhere to their project as set out in their proposal, even when it becomes obvious that a change in direction or focus is necessary or desirable.

WORK SMARTER

Do not be afraid to change the direction or focus of your research if it becomes apparent that this is necessary or desirable. Remember, it is the nature of research that it changes and evolves as you do it.

You should also remember that you are not expected to have the answers to your research questions – as set out in your proposal – at the start of your dissertation; in fact, if you did have the answers, there would be little point in doing the research.

9.7   METHODS, METHODOLOGY AND RESEARCH ETHICS

Students are often confused by the words 'methods' and 'methodology' as they apply to research. This confusion is not helped by the fact that the two words are sometimes (erroneously) used interchangeably. Strictly speaking, they mean different things, and your awareness of the difference will be useful when you undertake your research. Briefly put, methodology refers to the philosophical basis of your research; methods refer to the ways in which you collect and analyse your research data.

It is worth noting that, unlike some other subjects (e.g. sociology), it is reasonably common for those researching in law not to make reference to, or even consider, their methodology. You should take the advice of your supervisor when deciding whether it is appropriate for you to do so.

Ethical research requires all researchers to behave appropriately and ethically. This is particularly important for research that involves participants, such as interviewees or focus groups. You may be required to obtain ethical approval from your institution before you engage in certain types of research.

The following sections on methodologies, methods and ethics are introductory. If you wish to explicitly identify, and write about, your methodology and employ particular methods (such as interviews or use questionnaires) in your research, then you should consult some of the more specialist texts. Similarly, you should consult the relevant literature, including your institution's guidance, if your research is likely to need ethical approval.

9.7.1   Methodologies

When social science researchers talk about methodology, they are referring to the philosophical approach that guides you in the conduct and writing of your research.

Whenever you undertake research, you are – whether you are aware of it or not – approaching the subject matter of your enquiry from a particular point of view, from a particular perspective. To say the same thing in a different way: there is no such thing as a neutral approach in research. Your research will always be influenced by certain biases and prejudices, some of which you will be aware of and others which you will not.

These points about methodology have been eloquently expressed by Cryer *et al.*:

> Every legal research project begins from a theoretical basis or bases, whether such bases are articulated or not. The theoretical basis of a project will inform how law is conceptualised in the project, which in turn will determine what kinds of research questions are deemed meaningful or useful, what data is examined and how it is analysed (the method). Often these are arrived at unconsciously, usually on the basis of how a subject was taught to you, and/or what you gravitate towards naturally because it interests you. We believe, however, that it is better to be open about the bases of research and to think about them than to leave them unaddressed and uncritically accepted . . . For us, methodology has theoretical connotations. Moreover, methodology is closely related to what we understand the field of enquiry . . . to be. Methodology guides our thinking or questioning of, or within, that field or both.
>
> (R. Cryer, T. Hervey, and B. Sokhi-Bulley (2011) *Research Methodologies in EU and International Law*, Oxford, UK: Hart, pp. 4–5)

So, methodology provides the framework – for instance, in terms of context and language – with which you can begin and continue to understand, think about, discuss and write about the subject matter of your enquiry. It provides you with certain assumptions that help facilitate your understanding.

Given this, you can imagine that it is desirable that you are explicitly aware, and sometimes that you expressly refer to, your methodological approach. To do so gives your research a depth that it would otherwise lack. It also helps you to appreciate, and let your reader know you appreciate, that your research is limited; that someone else undertaking similar research, but using a different methodological approach, might reach different conclusions.

So, at the risk of oversimplifying, if you wanted to undertake a feminist critique of employment law, then the feminism aspect of your research would be the methodology: the philosophical basis of your enquiry that governs the types of question you wish to ask and how you proceed to answer them.

9.7.2   Methods

Whereas methodology refers to the philosophical approach taken when engaging in research, methods refers to the techniques used in gathering, analysing and processing data.

So, for instance, if you want to gather data using a questionnaire, then this would be your method, and similarly, if you want to use interviews or focus groups to obtain your data. It may be that you do not want to engage in such empirical research, but, rather, wish to analyse case law, legislation or academic literature (sometimes called desk-based, or library-based, research); if so, then this is your method: the way in which you are going to collect and analyse your data.

Being explicit about your methodology, and the methods employed, in any research project is good practice. It demonstrates a sophisticated understanding of the research process and of the limits of your research. It also allows your reader to make a judgment about the veracity of your conclusions. In fact, for some research projects, describing your methodology and the methods used allows others to test your work by attempting to reproduce your findings.

9.7.3   Qualitative, quantitative, black-letter and socio-legal research

In the social sciences, there are two main methodological approaches: qualitative and quantitative. In basic terms, qualitative research is concerned – in the main –

with the views, experiences and feelings of individuals, whereas quantitative research is concerned with gathering large amounts of data and using them to reach conclusions.

In legal research, it is common to talk of black-letter (sometimes known as doctrinal) and socio-legal research. Black-letter research attempts to analyse legislation, case law or even a particular theory about the law without reference to any 'non-legal' factors. It does not, then, take account of, say, political, social or economic considerations. As we will see, these, and other 'non-legal' factors are the very things that socio-legal research does examine.

Qualitative, quantitative, black-letter and socio-legal research are sometimes talked of as being different methodologies. This is because they are often associated with a particular philosophical view as to what amounts to valid knowledge or – when considering black-letter and socio-legal research – what amounts to valid legal knowledge. To illustrate, a socio-legal researcher might reject the assumption, which is sometimes ascribed to black-letter researchers, that law can be understood and analysed as though it were a discrete phenomenon, uninfluenced by political, societal or other factors.

However, I suggest that, rather than see qualitative/quantitative or black-letter/socio-legal as rival epistemological theories (i.e. theories about knowledge), it is better to consider them as different tools, each of which might be appropriate, depending on the nature of the research. For some projects, a black-letter approach might be most suitable, whereas, for others, a socio-legal approach might be best. Indeed, as we shall see, many projects will utilise a mixture of approaches.

9.7.3.1 Qualitative research

As stated above, qualitative research is concerned, in the main, with the views, experiences and feelings of individuals. Two examples might illustrate:

- *Example 1*: A colleague of mine conducted interviews with a small group of men to ascertain their experiences and feelings of fearing that their female partners or relatives might be the victims of crime.
- *Example 2*: A colleague and I interviewed one woman who had been stopped and had her car seized by the police. Among other things, we wanted to discover her feelings about the way she had been treated. We were able to use the information we gathered to make some criticisms of the police, their policies and their procedures.

This second example indicates some of the strengths of the qualitative approach. My colleague and I were able to spend time talking to our interviewee in depth and hearing and attempting to understand the full extent of her experiences. We were also able to ensure, as much as possible, that we accurately recorded her feelings and experiences, rather than imposing, or fitting them into, our own, ready-made structure. It may also have been a cathartic experience for her: she was able to talk about what had happened to her and explain the way it made her feel, with people who were interested in what she had to say.

The example also illustrates some potential weaknesses of the approach. We interviewed one woman and heard only her experience with the officers who had dealt with her on one occasion. We could not use our research to make wider claims: that her experience is common or uncommon. For the same reason, our research, and the qualitative approach, is more subjective than quantitative research.

However, it is not the case that one cannot generalise from qualitative research. This type of research tells us about the in-depth views of individuals and tells us something about life in general. This type of generalisation cannot be quantified, but this does not mean it is without value.

It should be apparent that qualitative research can be conducted in a number of ways, including interviews, focus groups, or ethnography or participant observation (where the researcher immerses him/herself within the group he/she is researching).

9.7.3.2 *Quantitative research*

Quantitative research operates differently from qualitative research. Here, the researcher is gathering large amounts of data in order to reach conclusions on the basis of the data obtained.

So, for instance, a research project that sought to establish whether people who were stopped by the police while driving were satisfied or dissatisfied with their treatment might take a quantitative approach. The researcher might use questionnaires to obtain information from a large number of individuals, in order to reach conclusions about what percentage of people felt they had been fairly dealt with. Of course, with research such as this, the number of participants has to be large enough so that the results say something meaningful about the way people feel they have been treated.

We can see, then, that one significant advantage of the quantitative approach is that we are able to reach conclusions that will be true for large groups of people. Also, because the result is based on a large amount of data, it has a degree of objectivity that is missing from qualitative research.

One of its weaknesses is that we lose some depth. For instance, contrary to the situation with a qualitative approach, we would not be able to record, or describe, the full experience of the participants in the research.

9.7.3.3 Black-letter research

The black-letter approach involves the deployment of the specialist technical skills of legal reasoning that are possessed by lawyers and those who have been legally educated. These legal skills allow lawyers to identify what the law requires in any particular case. The black-letter approach excludes policy considerations, economic considerations and acknowledgment of underlying ideologies (for instance, that law is capitalist or male-oriented) or other 'non-legal' factors. (I have put 'non-legal' in quotation marks because it is arguable that these factors – policy, society, economics and the like – are part and parcel of the law, rather than something separate and distinct.)

Black-letter research may be used in various ways. For example, a researcher may rely on decided cases to identify the principles underlying an area of law, say using decided cases to identify the principles governing the granting of permission in judicial review cases. Black-letter research may also be used to criticise a particular decision for being out of line with other decided cases.

9.7.3.4 Socio-legal studies

Socio-legal research does not try to examine law as an independent, discrete phenomenon. Rather, it commonly seeks to identify the (often unacknowledged) factors that influence the creation, development or application of the law.

So, socio-legal researchers may:

- research the law from a feminist perspective, to try to identify those influences that militate against the interests of women;
- seek to identify economic influences on the development of the law;
- seek to identify other social or political influences that are often hidden but that condition the way the law operates, is applied or is understood.

The last bullet point – that socio-legal researchers may attempt to identify the way in which the law operates, is applied or is understood – is important. It is well recognised that socio-legal research is a broad church. Those engaged in such research do not necessarily confine themselves to the way in which lawyers or judges operate. They may be interested in the views and actions of other legal actors, such as the police or jury members, or non-legal actors. For example, a socio-legal researcher may seek to elicit how those engaged in criminal activity view their relationships with the police.

Those undertaking socio-legal research will adopt the research methods of the social sciences, including the qualitative and quantitative approaches described already. Such researchers may acknowledge, and seek to identify, the ideological and other influences that condition the way the law operates in reality.

9.7.3.5 Mixed-methods research

It will often be appropriate to use a mixture of qualitative and quantitative, or black-letter and socio-legal, approaches when undertaking research.

A simple example of a mixed-methods approach might be where a researcher uses a questionnaire delivered to large numbers of people (i.e. a quantitative approach) to decide who would be suitable respondents to be interviewed (a qualitative approach).

A slightly different approach might be one where the researcher uses a quantitative approach to obtain broad data and a qualitative approach to drill down and obtain some depth. So, let's say that I wanted to find out how police officers understand a change in the criminal law: I might use a questionnaire to get large amounts of information and use semi-structured interviews with a few officers to get more depth.

A third example might be where a researcher uses one methodology to corroborate the findings obtained via another. For example, you might engage in participant observation of, say, those engaged in football violence, which leads to some conclusions about loyalty to a football team (i.e. a qualitative approach), a conclusion that you then test with a large-scale questionnaire asking questions of football fans in general (i.e. a quantitative approach).

Likewise, a researcher may use both black-letter and socio-legal research in one project. For instance, a researcher might use a black-letter approach to identify the principles inherent in an area of law and then criticise this from a socio-legal perspective.

9.7.4   Research ethics

In recent years, higher-education institutions and other bodies concerned with research have taken more of an interest in ensuring that those who research do so ethically.

Broadly speaking, ethical research requires, as a minimum, that you, as researcher, do no physical or psychological harm, either to those whom you research or yourself. It may also require that you take positive steps to maintain the well-being of the participants in your research, for instance, by making provision for access to a counsellor for those being interviewed about sensitive matters. You will also be expected to act lawfully at all times while researching.

It is likely that you will require ethical approval before you undertake any research that involves you interacting with others: for instance, before you interview people or gather information by questionnaire. Indeed, doing such research before you obtain ethical approval may be considered by your institution to be a form of academic malpractice, which may lead to disciplinary action.

Moreover, the requirements of ethical research will usually oblige you to fully inform your participants (say, your interviewees) of the nature of your project, to acquire their consent and to give them the opportunity to withdraw from the research at any point up until near to the completion of your project. Depending on the nature of your research, you may additionally be required to anonymise the participants in your research and to store securely any data obtained. In brief, as a researcher, you are expected to treat your research participants with dignity and respect.

Given the above, it is very likely that your institution may not grant ethical approval for certain kinds of research. In addition, in some situations, ethical approval may be denied for an undergraduate project where it would be granted if undertaken by an experienced researcher. So, it is unlikely that an undergraduate would be given approval to engage in covert research or in research with vulnerable individuals or in dangerous situations.

It is very likely that your institution has produced some guidance about research ethics, about when approval will be required and about how you may acquire such approval. Your supervisor will also be able to advise you on these matters.

9.8   YOU AND YOUR SUPERVISOR

The relationship you have with your dissertation supervisor is very important, and you should do all you can to ensure that it is cordial and productive.

For a start, you must make sure that you take the opportunity to meet and receive feedback and advice from your supervisor. If you do not, your dissertation may not attain the marks it would otherwise get.

LECTURERS' THOUGHTS	
Anna	'Often, students don't make the most of the opportunity for supervision. You don't see them all year and then they submit a dissertation that is sub-standard and you think, "Well, there's a missed opportunity".'

Furthermore, you must adhere closely to the advice given by your supervisor; indeed, their advice trumps all other advice you might receive about your dissertation, including the advice contained in this book.

Sometimes, students wish to go their own way and not follow the suggestions of their supervisor. This is understandable in some ways. Your dissertation is your project, and you, as a student, might have very strong ideas about how it should be undertaken and a strong sense of ownership, and you may be very protective of it. However, remember:

- Your supervisor will probably know much better than you what is required to successfully complete your project and get the best marks.
- Your overall aim is to get the best marks possible.
- It is very likely that your supervisor will be the person marking your dissertation (and so it would be foolish not to do it in the way they think best).

There are different ways in which you can work with your dissertation supervisor, and you should take your lead from them, asking them how they prefer to work, if necessary. The commonest way to work with supervisors is to send them drafts of your work (say, a draft chapter) and then have a follow-up meeting at which you discuss the work you sent. The following advice assumes that, generally speaking, this is how you will work with your supervisor.

The first piece of advice is that any work you send to your supervisor should be as near to the completed article as you can make it; even though it is in draft, you should make sure that it is as well written as possible, in terms of grammar, structure, spelling, whether it makes sense, and its general presentation. There are two main reasons for this. First, your supervisor will soon tire of having to correct remedial errors that you should have eliminated before the work came anywhere near them. Second, you are not making the best use of your time with your supervisor if they are spending their time amending such simple errors. Indeed, on occasions, I have been presented with draft chapters by my dissertation students that have been so poorly written and structured that my only advice could be for the students to rewrite them so that they made sense.

LECTURERS' PET HATES

'A pet hate of mine is students not proofreading work before submitting it to supervisors for comment. The role of the supervisor is to comment on structure and content rather than [correcting] elementary errors.'

When sending your draft chapters to your supervisor, remember, they will not be as familiar with your work as you are. Indeed, your lecturers will often be supervising other research projects – both undergraduate and postgraduate – and may not fully remember the details of yours or what you decided at your last meeting together. Given this, you will get the best out of your supervisor if, when you send them your draft work, you also include:

- a brief précis of your overall project;
- what the chapter (or part chapter) you have sent contributes to the project; and
- where relevant, a summary of any previous advice you have received in relation to the chapter.

So, if you send your work by email, it might read as shown in Figure 9.2.

WORK SMARTER

Whenever you send draft work through to your supervisor, include a brief summary of your overall project, as a reminder, and what the work you have sent contributes to your overall thesis.

To: Simon Smartypants
From: Timothy Timid
Subject: Chapter 3 of my dissertation

Dear Simon

I hope you are well.

Please find attached a draft of chapter 3 of my dissertation. Just to remind you, my project attempts to answer the question of whether the rationales offered by the courts to justify the different aspects of judicial review are conflicting. Chapter 2, which you have previously seen, examined the permission stage, time limits and sufficient interest and suggested that the rationale offered for each is to protect government bodies from undue interference. The attached chapter examines the grounds for judicial review and suggests that governmental bodies are held to a more demanding standard than private bodies.

I look forward to hearing from you to arrange our next meeting to discuss the attached.

Best wishes

Tim.

Figure 9.2 Example email accompanying draft work

When attempting to arrange a supervisory meeting with your supervisor, attempt to be as flexible as possible. It is little use, for example, informing them that you can only meet on Tuesdays at 3.30 p.m., if that is the very time that they will be taking a lecture. Any lack of flexibility on your part about meeting may be reciprocated.

Whenever you do meet your supervisor, you should make a careful note of the advice that they offer. If necessary, you should ask them to clarify something you do not fully understand.

Immediately after each supervisory meeting, you should take some time to think and read over the information you have received, to ensure you understand it and to help you remember, making additional notes if necessary. It is fairly common for students to fully understand the advice they received when they hear it, but to forget exactly what was said when they next come to work on their dissertation, which may be a day or two later.

9.9 WRITING THE DISSERTATION

The following sections will provide advice about the different components that commonly make up dissertations. You should also consult other sections of this book; in particular, you should look at:

- Section 6.4.2 of Chapter 6 for advice about planning your work;
- Section 6.7 of Chapter 6 for advice about proofreading your work; and
- Chapter 10 for advice about referencing, bibliographies, lists of cases, tables of legislation and using quotations.

It is common for dissertations to contain the elements shown in Table 9.2 (take advice from your supervisor about what should be included in your work).

9.9.1 Title page

The title page may provide:

- the title of the thesis;
- your name (though there may be a requirement that your dissertation is anonymised for marking purposes);
- the name of the supervisor;
- the date of submission;
- the name of your institution;
- the module code for the dissertation;
- the degree that you are doing.

There may be rules governing the content of the title page and what it should contain; as ever, you should seek the advice of your supervisor as to what should be included and how it should be formatted.

9.9.2 Abstract

An abstract is a brief summary of the argument made in the dissertation. Its purpose is to provide the reader with a brief overview of the project. The length of abstracts varies, and your institution may specify a word limit for them, but they are often between 300 and 500 words. You should ask your supervisor whether you should include an abstract with your dissertation.

Table 9.2 Elements often found in dissertations

Element	Description
Title page	A page giving, among other things, the title of the thesis and the author's name (though check whether your work should be anonymised). There may be specific requirements governing how your title page should be set out and what it should contain
Abstract	A brief précis outlining the argument made in the dissertation
Contents page	A page listing the chapters, and sometimes the subheadings in each chapter, that make up the dissertation and the pages on which they may be found
Introduction	A chapter giving the reader a brief introductory overview of the work and details of each of the chapters
Literature review	The literature review provides a critical account of the existing literature in the area of study and, ideally, indicates a gap in the existing work that your dissertation will fill. The literature review may be a separate chapter or woven through the whole dissertation
Conclusion	A chapter that sums up the overall argument of the dissertation
Bibliography	Either: a list of all the texts consulted when writing the dissertation or a list only of the texts referred to in the dissertation. You should ask your supervisor what is required. Also, see Chapter 10 for advice about bibliographies
Appendices	Appendices are often used to include work that you may refer to in the main body of your dissertation but that is not a part of the dissertation. For instance, an appendix may contain: • statistical data to which you refer in the dissertation; • interview transcripts; • relevant email exchanges

LLB3001 Dissertation

The University of Brilliant Minds

CONFLICTING RATIONALES: JUDICIAL REVIEW AND ITS UNDERLYING PRINCIPLES

By Timothy Timid

Submitted 1st May 2015

Supervisor: Professor Simon Smartypants

Figure 9.3 Example title page

TIP BOX

You will often find abstracts at the start of journal articles. Read over a few of these to get an idea of what is required.

Given that you want your abstract to accurately reflect your work, it should be one of the last things that you write.

9.9.3   The introduction, chapters and conclusion

The introduction

Ideally, your introduction should give the reader an indication of what they are about to read (without giving so much away that there is little point in reading the thing – not always an easy thing to do) and make it clear why the subject matter of your dissertation is worthy of interest (again, not always easy).

You can begin with a paragraph or two setting the context – the background – of your dissertation. This might, for instance, be by reference to legislation or a particular judicial decision that appears to alter the area of law that you are going to investigate. Alternatively, you might explain that the area of law you wish to examine has been the subject of recent academic scrutiny. Giving this context will mean that your reader understands the backdrop of your research and begins to see why it is of interest.

Next, you need to give a more detailed overview of what your dissertation is about; again, however, you need to be careful not to give so much away that your reader need not continue reading.

Finally, you should give a brief outline of each of the chapters that compose the dissertation; once again, though, you should not give so much detail that reading the dissertation is pointless or would be a chore.

Because your introduction needs to reflect the contents of the dissertation accurately, writing it should – like the abstract – be one of the last jobs that you do.

The chapters

Your dissertation will be made up of three or four chapters (in addition to the introduction and conclusion); the appropriate number of chapters depends on the length of your dissertation.

You should see each chapter as a piece – a building block – of the overall argument that your dissertation makes. Each should naturally follow from those that precede it.

Each chapter should have an introductory paragraph or two, indicating what the reader is about to read. Each chapter should also have a conclusion summarising the contents of the chapter and, where appropriate, giving a sentence or two leading into the next chapter.

It is usual, in dissertations, to use headings and subheadings to break up your chapters and, in this way, make your work more accessible for your reader.

The conclusion

The purpose of the concluding chapter is to summarise the dissertation as a whole, though you should try to do this without being repetitive. You might also want to use the conclusion to explain the contribution your work makes to the existing literature and to suggest any future research that naturally leads from your thesis.

9.9.4 The literature review

When researching and writing any research project, you must undertake a review of the existing literature. This is a critical account of the existing literature in the subject area of your research. So, if you want to examine the law of joint enterprise in criminal law, you need to give an overview of the existing literature written about the subject. However, your account has to be critical – you are not simply describing the current thought in the area: you are also making an evaluation of it.

As noted above, your literature review should either be a separate chapter or be woven through your dissertation as a whole. The latter approach is appropriate when, for instance, your project is focused on examining some theoretical arguments made in the literature and you wish to draw on different aspects of existing work at different points in your dissertation. So, whether your literature review should exist as a separate chapter or not depends on the nature of your project, and you should ask your supervisor's advice.

The literature review has three main functions. First, it demonstrates your understanding of, and engagement with, the existing literature. Second, it sites your research within the context of the existing work on the subject. Finally, and ideally, it shows the contribution that your dissertation is making to existing thought by demonstrating the gap that your work will fill.

Table 9.3 What a literature review should be

Not a summary of individual texts	Rather, a thematic account that identifies common themes throughout the literature
'Professor Smartypants, in his article, 'Submit to sufficient interest', examines some of the reasons given for the sufficient interest requirement and argues that its primary function is to restrict access to the courts'	'The existing literature suggests that some of the procedural aspects of judicial review are often explained as a means of rationalising the supervisory jurisdiction. Smartypants contends that this is the primary reason given for the sufficient interest requirement: that it restricts access to the courts. Cleverclogs makes a similar argument with regard to the short time limit in judicial review: that, in effect, it protects government bodies from claims being brought long after the decision being challenged, thereby reducing the number of judicial claims that may be brought'
'Dr Cleverclogs, in his article 'Timing', describes some of the reasons provided for the short time limit in judicial review. He suggests that each of them amounts to an argument that decisions of governmental bodies should not be subject to judicial supervision after a certain length of time'	

The literature review should be thematic: that is, it should not be simply a summary of the different articles or books that have been written on a subject. Rather, it should be a (critical) account of the themes that run through the literature.

Although your literature review should be thematic, it is often a good idea to start constructing your review by writing a brief summary of each existing relevant text. You can then use these to gain an overview of the existing literature and to start to draw out some of the dominant themes.

9.9.5   The title

Students sometimes struggle to devise an adequate title for their dissertation. Generally speaking, your title should be (reasonably) short, snappy and accurate. It should not be overly long or descriptive.

So, for example, the following title would be accurate but would be much too long and descriptive:

> *An Examination, and Comparison, of the Different Rationales Given for the Sufficient Interest Requirement, Time Limits, Permission Stage and Grounds in Judicial Review Cases and an Argument that these Rationales Conflict.*

Indeed, such a laboured and ponderous title would make any reader's heart sink, because they might assume it presages a similar dissertation (and, if they have a choice, they may decide that life is too short to read it). It would be better as:

> *Conflicting Rationales: Judicial Review and Its Underlying Principles*

Often, people give their work a title that is a pun or play on words. So, for example, the following article title is based on one of the most famous works by the legal theorist Ronald Dworkin – *Law's Empire* – and a film in the Star Wars franchise:

> 'Dworkin's Empire Strikes Back!' (by J.A. Corlette in *The Statute Law Review* (2000) 21 (1): 43–56)

In trying to come up with a suitable title for your dissertation, you might find it beneficial to look at some journal articles to see the types of title adopted by established academics.

9.10   MANAGING YOUR TIME

One of the difficulties many students have when undertaking a dissertation is with managing their time. There are a number of reasons for this.

Some students find it difficult to operate outside the concrete structure provided by regular, timetabled classes, with the subject parameters, and any coursework questions, set by the lecturers. Often, such students do not thrive in the flexible conditions under which a dissertation is produced.

Also, a dissertation is usually a year-long project: commonly, a student begins at the start of their final year and submits it at the end. Because of this, it is tempting to prioritise other work that needs to be submitted throughout the year – say, coursework for other modules – and to continually put the dissertation on the back burner. Moreover, this potential problem might be compounded by the fact that your dissertation supervisor might not see it as their job to ensure you are diligently working on your project.

One way to try to combat the problem of allowing your other work to crowd out, and take priority over, your dissertation is to produce a timetable. This should be a realistic estimation of when you will produce the different components of your dissertation. When drafting such a timetable, keep in mind the following principles:

- You should first put in place the submission date for your dissertation and for any coursework that you will need to complete.
- You should take into account anything else that might be a significant draw on your time; this might be, for instance: the lead-up to any exams (when you might want to be revising); any employment commitments you might have (particularly if there are times of the year when you will be particularly busy); and any family commitments.
- For each chapter, you should factor into your calculations that you will want to produce a draft of the chapter and receive feedback on it from your supervisor, which you then work into the final version.

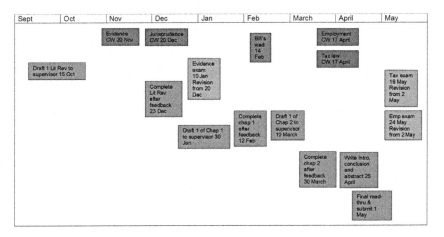

Figure 9.4 Example timetable

Constructing such a timetable may help you keep abreast of your dissertation throughout the year, rather than allowing it to be crowded out by other things. At the very least, it will probably give you a feeling of continuing guilt if you slip behind, which may, in turn, motivate you to keep engaged with it.

Chapter 10
Referencing and bibliography

This chapter will discuss:

- the importance of referencing;
- how to reference, including dealing with repeat references;
- the appropriate way to refer to cases in your writing;
- the use of square and round brackets in citations;
- what is required in a bibliography;
- when and how to use quotations.

10.1 INTRODUCTION

As noted in Chapters 3 and 6, it is extremely important that your work is informed by academic commentary, and that you substantiate your arguments by reference to such commentary and, more importantly, to relevant case law and legislative authority.

10.2 THE IMPORTANCE OF REFERENCING

As lawyers, and law students, it is not enough simply to state what you think the law is: you need to be able to prove what the law is, or at least make a strong argument that the law requires one thing rather than another.

That is, it is not enough simply to state, for example, that the law requires that those who injure another through their negligence should be liable to pay compensation for that injury. As lawyers – and probably even more so as law students – you should provide the legal evidence to back up any such claims. Lawyers call this 'legal authority' or simply 'authority'.

'Authority', in this context, refers to the judicial decision, legislation or other source used to substantiate (i.e. to provide evidence for) a proposition of law.

For example, the case of *Donoghue v Stevenson* [1932] AC 562 provides the authority for the legal proposition that you are under an obligation not to injure those who you could reasonably foresee might be injured by your negligent act.

There are a number of reasons why you should provide this legal authority, including the following:

1   Let us imagine that you are a practising lawyer acting on behalf of your client in court; you may want to provide a judge with some legal evidence as to why she should decide that the law favours your client's case rather than your opponent's. Likewise, as a law student, you will want to provide the marker of your coursework with the evidence that the law is what you claim it to be.
2   It is often not clear what the law requires in a particular situation. So, again, you may be trying to persuade a judge, or the marker of your coursework, that the law is what you claim and you may be relying on legal authority to do this.
3   A law degree is an academic degree, and academics in general are expected, where possible, to provide evidence for the claims they make. Academic lawyers provide legal evidence for their claims.

The reason why academics reference is that it enables those who read – or who mark – their work to check the validity of what is being argued. Also, it is a requirement of academic courtesy that academics acknowledge the source of their arguments.

That is not to say that you must provide a reference for every contention you make. It is appropriate – in fact, as a student, it is positively desirable – that you make your own independent arguments and, in such cases, you do not need to provide authority. I emphasise this point because I have had students who believe that they cannot make an argument unless they are able to substantiate it with some authority. Yet, even where you make your own, independent arguments, they may be influenced by, or an adaptation of, someone else's, and, if they are, it is necessary to acknowledge the fact.

The references in your work, along with the bibliography, may be used by your marker as an indication of the amount of work you have undertaken to complete the coursework. You should, therefore, ensure that you fully reference all the sources on which you have relied.

In addition, your taking the time and making the effort to reference correctly may be used by your marker as an indication of how seriously you take your work. Indeed, as noted in Section 6.2 of Chapter 6, three of the lecturers I asked about marking specifically said that one of the factors they consider is whether the referencing is correct.

LECTURERS' THOUGHTS	
Anna	'When marking coursework, I ask myself . . . is it well written, well presented and *correctly referenced*?'
Bill	'Are the *referencing and bibliography correct*?'
David	'I also look at the *clarity* and *correctness* of the *footnotes and the referencing*.'

This suggests a further reason why you, as a student, should take referencing seriously: in a borderline case, the correctness and accuracy of your referencing might make the difference between one grade and another (e.g. between a first-class mark and a 2:1, between a 2:1 and a 2:2, etc.).

LECTURERS' PET HATES
'Students not bothering to get their referencing right is a real pet hate of mine. I can understand new students struggling at first, but after a while I start to think that they simply can't be bothered to get it right.'

LECTURERS' THOUGHTS	
Anna	'Referencing is not difficult, it just takes practice and attention to detail. Because it's something you can get right, it's infuriating to see students making simple errors in their third year, say.'

10.3   HOW TO REFERENCE

It is very likely that your law school will supply you with detailed guidance about how to reference. This will be either its own system (its 'house style') or one that is generally available. With regard to the latter, use of the Oxford University Standard for Citation of Legal Authorities (OSCOLA) is becoming more common. This can be found at: www.law.ox.ac.uk/publications/oscola.php

These guides will provide you with direction about various aspects of referencing, including:

- how to refer to various authorities (e.g. how to refer to legislation; whether case names should be italicised; how to cite books (e.g. the order to state the author, date of publication, title and publisher) and journal articles);
- how to deal with repeat references (i.e. where you refer more than once to the same authority in your work); and
- use of Latin terms.

Whichever referencing style your law school prescribes, you must make sure that you fully and consistently adhere to it. In fact, if you can, it is a good idea to obtain a hard copy of your school's referencing guide and keep it to hand for consultation whenever you are writing. If there is something that you are unsure of with regard to referencing, seek advice from one of your lecturers.

TIP BOX

The watchword for successful referencing is consistency. Whichever referencing style you use, you must make sure that the way you reference is uniform throughout your work.

10.3.1 Repeat references

Often, you will want to refer to the same case, journal article or book more than once in your work. With regard to such repeat references, you will not normally be required to repeat the reference in full each time you cite it. Rather, your law school's referencing guide will most likely instruct you how to cross-reference later citations of the same case or text back to the first time you used it.

Table 10.1 Repeat references

Don't repeat each reference in full each time you use it
[1] Craig, P.P., 'Legislative Intent and Legislative Supremacy: A Reply to Professor Allen' (2004) 24(4) *Oxford Journal of Legal Studies* 585, 590.
[2] Dworkin, R. (1998) *Law's Empire*, Oxford: Hart Publishing, p. 225.
[3] Dworkin, R. (1998) *Law's Empire*, Oxford: Hart Publishing, p. 225.
[4] Dworkin, R. (1998) *Law's Empire*, Oxford: Hart Publishing, p. 200.
[5] Craig, P.P., 'Legislative Intent and Legislative Supremacy: A Reply to Professor Allen' (2004) 24(4) *Oxford Journal of Legal Studies* 585, 589.
Cross-reference later citations back to the first instance of their use (your law school's referencing guide will instruct you on how to do this)
[1] Craig, P.P., 'Legislative Intent and Legislative Supremacy: A Reply to Professor Allen' (2004) 24(4) *Oxford Journal of Legal Studies* 585, 590.
[2] Dworkin, R. (1998) *Law's Empire*, Oxford: Hart Publishing, p. 225.
[3] Ibid.
[4] Ibid, p. 200.
[5] Craig, op. cit., p. 589, above n. 1.

You will notice that, in Table 10.1, some Latin abbreviations – 'ibid.' and 'op. cit.' – have been used. Your law school's referencing guide will instruct you about whether, and when, such Latin terms should be employed. Table 10.2 gives some advice about the meaning and use of the commonest.

When dealing with repeat references, you will often be cross-referencing to other footnotes or pages in your work. Given this, you should provide all references in full when writing your work and make the cross-referencing one of the last tasks that you perform. The reason for this is that, otherwise, you may insert new references during the writing process, with the possible result that your cross-references will not match up.

10.3.2 Mentioning case law and other authorities

When using case law as authority, it will not normally be appropriate to give the facts of the case. The exception to this is where the facts of the case are

Table 10.2 Latin terms, abbreviations, meaning and usage

Latin term	Abbreviation	Meaning	Usage
Ibid.	ibidem	In the same place	Used to refer to work cited in the immediately preceding reference
Op. cit.	opere citato	In the work previously cited	Used to refer to a work cited earlier in the text but not the immediately preceding reference
supra	–	Above	Used to refer to a work cited earlier (usually accompanied by a page or footnote number where the earlier work can be found)
infra	–	Below	Used to refer to a work that will be cited later (usually accompanied by a page or footnote number where the later work can be found)

necessary to demonstrate the point you are making (e.g. if you want to demonstrate how the facts of the problem question you are answering differ from a case you are citing). On such occasions, you only need to give sufficient facts as required to make your point.

In other situations, what is necessary is a matter of judgment governed by the situation. Where, for instance, you are using a case that is the obvious authority for a proposition of law – because, say, it is a well-known authority for that proposition or because the proposition is obviously part of the *ratio decidendi* – then you can usually simply provide the case name and citation in a footnote as per the example in Figure 10.1.

Where you are providing a reference for a quotation, or referring to a point made in a particular place in a judgment, then you should give the page(s) of the law report – or, if they are numbered, the paragraph number(s) – from where the quotation is taken or the point may be found. This is sometimes known as giving

When determining whether a defendant incurs liability for their negligent acts, the courts make use of a number of principles. First, they will ask whether the defendant could have reasonably foreseen that their negligent act would lead to the damage caused.[1] If the answer to this question is yes, the courts will then ask

---

1. *Donoghue v Stevenson* [1932] AC 562

Figure 10.1 Example of simple case citation

Recent years have seen the enactment of the Constitutional Reform Act 2005 and judicial statements that the United Kingdom has "constitutional" statutes[1] and "constitutional arrangements".[2] Despite these developments, it would seem that the question of whether the United Kingdom has a constitution is one which has yet to receive a conclusive answer.

At its most basic, a constitution may be defined as "a set of rules which governs an organisation".[3] Other definitions may be more demanding. For instance, Ridley has stated that there are "essential characteristics" that a constitution should have.[4]

---

1. *Thoburn v Sunderland City Council* [2003] Q.B. 151, paragraphs 60 & 62.
2. *R (Jackson and Others) v Attorney General* [2005] QB 579, paragraph 48.
3. Barnett, H. (2004) *Constitutional and Administrative Law.* 5th ed., London: Cavendish Publishing, p. 6.
4. Ridley, F. F., "There is no British Constitution: a dangerous case of the Emperor's New Clothes" (1988) 41 *Parliamentary Affairs* 340, pp. 342-343.

Figure 10.2 Pinpoint references

the pinpoint reference. The same principle applies when making use of academic authorities: you should supply the particular page numbers of any book or journal article to which you are referring.

Moreover, to repeat the advice I gave in Section 3.2.1 of Chapter 3, when referencing a case, or relying on it as authority, you should cite the case directly, rather than rely on some secondary source such as a textbook that mentions that case.

LECTURERS' PET HATES

'The other thing that annoys me is referencing a case from a textbook. Do they imagine that the Supreme Court relies on textbooks?'

Correct – citing the primary source directly

> *Donoghue v Stevenson*[1] makes it clear that, when determining whether a defendant incurs liability for their negligent act, the courts will make use of a number of principles. First, they will ask
>
> -----
>
> [1.] [1932] AC 562

Incorrect – citing a secondary source rather than the primary

> The case of *Donoghue v Stevenson*[1] makes it clear that, when determining whether a defendant incurs liability for their negligent act, the courts will make use of a number of principles. First, they will ask
>
> -----
>
> [1.] C Elliott and F Quinn (2003) *Tort Law*, 4th ed., Harlow: Pearson, p. 15.

Figure 10.3 Correct and incorrect citations

10.3.3 **Square and round brackets**

You may have noticed that, for the citations of both cases and journal articles, sometimes the year of the case report or journal is in round brackets and sometimes in square. Look at the following two case citations, for instance, both for the *Thoburn* case:

   Thoburn v Sunderland City Council [2003] QB 151

   Thoburn v Sunderland City Council (2002) 166 JP 257

These both refer to the same case, as reported in different law reports: the first is in the Queen's Bench Law Reports; the second is in the Justice of the Peace

Reports. The interesting question for present purposes is why the date of the first is in square brackets and that of the second in round. There is a reason.

You will notice that the second citation has a number between the date and the initials of the report: 166. This means that the case may be found in Volume 166 of the Justice of the Peace Reports. It just so happens that the volume number of these reports increases year on year, so that:

- 166 was the volume number for the year 2002;
- 167 was the volume number for the year 2003;
- 168 was the volume number for the year 2004, and so on.

What this means is that you can find the correct volume number without reference to the year of publication, and this is why the year is in round brackets.

Where the year is in square brackets, this means that you need the year in which the law report in question was published in order to find the correct volume.

The same applies to journals. If the date of publication is in square brackets, this means that you need the date to find the correct volume. If the date is in round brackets, then the date is not crucial: you can find the correct volume using either the date or the volume number.

So, for instance, in the following example, the correct volume of the journal *Parliamentary Affairs* for the cited article may be found by either the date or the volume number, and so the date is in round brackets:

F.F. Ridley 'There is no British Constitution: A Dangerous Case of the Emperor's New Clothes' (1988) 41 *Parliamentary Affairs* 340

In the next example, however, the date is necessary in order to find the correct volume of the journal *Public Law* and so it is in square brackets:

A. Tucker 'Constitutional Writing and Constitutional Rights' [2013] PL 345.

These distinctions are becoming less important, given that most lawyers and law students will access electronic versions of these reports or journal articles rather than hard copies in a law library. However, you should still cite in the correct way. If in doubt, the journal or law report may indicate how it should be cited; alternatively, you can look to see how they are cited on Westlaw or LexisNexis or in textbooks.

I should note two final points about volume numbers. First, you may get a volume number and a date in square brackets, for example:

> *R (on the application of Jackson) v Attorney General* [2005] 3 WLR 733

This means that the case may be found in Volume 3 of the Weekly Law Reports of 2005. Here, the volume number does not provide an alternative way to identify the year of publication; it is simply the third volume of 2005. Consequently, the date is in square brackets because it is needed to find the correct volume.

Second, you will sometimes see an additional number, usually in brackets, beside the volume number, for both law reports and journal articles, as you can see in the following citation for an (excellent) article by your modest author:

> J. McGarry 'The Principle of Parliamentary Sovereignty' (2012) 32(4) *Legal Studies* 577

Here, the article may be found in Volume 32 of the journal *Legal Studies*. The '4' in brackets after the volume number refers to the issue number – there are four issues to each volume of *Legal Studies*, and the article can be found in Issue 4 of Volume 32.

10.3.4 To italicise or not

You will notice in the different examples in this chapter that case names, book titles and the full titles of journals are written in italics, whereas the titles of academic articles and legislation are not. Your law school's referencing guide will specify how you should write these different things, but the following (based on OSCOLA) is common.

- Book titles are normally written in italics:
  M. Kelman, *A Guide to Critical Legal Studies* (Cambridge, Mass. Harvard University Press 1987)
- The title of journal articles is normally given in single or double quotation marks:
  A. Tucker 'Constitutional Writing and Constitutional Rights' [2013] PL 345
- If the journal title is written out in full, it is in italics:
  J. McGarry 'The Principle of Parliamentary Sovereignty' (2012) 32(4) *Legal Studies* 577

- Case names are written in italics, and the citation is in regular font:
  R (on the application of Jackson) v Attorney General [2005] 3 WLR 733
- Legislation is written in normal font:
  The Human Rights Act 1998.

10.4   BIBLIOGRAPHY

You will usually be required to provide a bibliography for your coursework. You will almost certainly be required to provide one if you write a dissertation. These are a record of the texts – e.g. journal articles and books – you have used in your coursework. They are arranged alphabetically, according to the authors' surnames, and usually come at the end of your work.

There are two basic types:

1   a record of only the texts to which you have made reference in your work; or
2   a record of all the texts to which you have referred in, as well as those that you have consulted to write, your work.

Bibliography

Barnett, H. (2004) *Constitutional and Administrative Law*, 5th ed., London: Cavendish Publishing

Bradley, A. W. and Ewing, K. D. (2003) *Constitutional and Administrative Law*, 13th ed., Harlow: Longman

Calvert, H. (1985) *An Introduction to British Constitutional Law*, London: Financial Training

Corsianos, G. "The Constitution of the United Kingdom?" (2001) 6 *Queen Mary Law Journal* 52

Dicey, A. V. (1959) *An Introduction to the Study of the Law of the Constitution*, 10th ed., London: Macmillan

Fenwick, H and Phillipson, G. (2003) *Text, Cases and Materials on Public Law & Human Rights*, 2nd ed., London: Cavendish Publishing Ltd

Jennings, I. (1959) *The Law and the Constitution*, 5th ed., London: Hodder & Staunton

Ridley, F. F., "There is no British Constitution: a dangerous case of the Emperor's New Clothes" (1988) 41 *Parliamentary Affairs* 340

Tomkins, A. (2003) *Public Law*, Oxford: Oxford University Press

---

Figure 10.4 Example bibliography

Whether a bibliography is required for coursework, and, if so, which type, will no doubt be detailed in your law school's legal referencing guide. If not, seek advice from your lecturers.

It may be that you are expected to list books and journal articles separately, or it may be that they are listed together; again, you should consult your referencing guide or ask one of your lecturers to clarify what is required. Figure 10.4 shows an example of a bibliography (where the books and journal articles are not separated).

You might also be expected to provide a list of cases and a table of legislation to accompany your work. As above, you should consult your law school's referencing guide, or ask one of your lecturers, to find out if this is necessary.

LIST OF CASES

Attorney General of Hong Kong v Ng Yuen Shiu [1983] 2 AC 629

Boddington v British Transport Police [1999] 2 AC 143

Council of Civil Service Unions v Minister for the Civil Service [1985] AC 374

Duport Steel v Sirs [1980] 1 WLR 142

Ellen St Estates v Minister of Health [1934] KB 590

Ghaidan v Godin-Mendoza [2004] UKHL 30

Hardy v Pembrokeshire CC [2006] Env LR 28

Macarthys v Smith [1979] ICR 785

TABLE OF LEGISLATION

Primary legislation

Constitutional Reform Act 2005

Human Rights Act 1998

Merchant Shipping Act 1988

Senior Courts Act 1981

Secondary legislation

The Civil Procedure Rules 1998 (SI 1998/3132)

The Justices' Allowance Regulations 2015 (SI 2015/1423)

The Solicitors (Disciplinary Proceedings) Rules 2007 (SI 2007/3588)

Figure 10.5 Example list of cases and table of legislation

A list of cases is simply a record of the cases, organised alphabetically, to which you have referred in your work. Similarly, a table of legislation details the legislation that has been cited. The pieces of legislation may be grouped together or separated into different categories, such as primary legislation, secondary legislation and international legislation or treaties.

10.5   USE OF QUOTATIONS

At times, it will be appropriate for you to use quotations in your work. You must, however, avoid the overuse of quotations. Indeed, you should use them infrequently; remember, your marker wants to read your work, not other people's simply collated and linked together by you. Your work should be a good balance of your thoughts and ideas, other people's contentions as paraphrased (restated) by you and some quotations. If you do paraphrase, make sure that you are not simply changing a few words – rather, that you articulate the argument in your own words – and that you fully acknowledge, with appropriate references, that the ideas you write about are another's.

You will get a good sense of when it is appropriate, or even necessary, to quote, through your reading of secondary materials. Generally speaking, and keeping in mind my warning against overusing quotations, you should consider quoting:

- at appropriate points when you judge that it would be better to quote the original rather than attempting to paraphrase; or
- when it will be useful for your reader to have the direct quotation so as better to understand your analysis or critique of it.

Generally speaking, any quotation you employ should be a faithful reproduction of the original. If you do make any changes, you must make these apparent to your reader in the following ways:

- *Square brackets*: If you add anything, say, to make the quotation read more grammatically or to better fit or make better sense in the context in which you are using it – in the context of your surrounding text – then you place the additional text in square brackets. You might also place square brackets around the first letter of a quotation if you have capitalised it for your use but the original was lower case.
- *Ellipses*: If you remove any text, either to improve the meaning in context or to remove parts of the quotation that are not necessary for the point you are making, you indicate this to your reader with the use of an ellipsis: three dots.

Both these methods can be seen in the following Lecturers' Pet Hates feature: I quote my colleague Carol and add some text in square brackets and use an ellipsis to remove some, so that the quotation makes better sense in context.

LECTURERS' PET HATES

'I hate irrelevance, for example [a student writing] "This is a question about land law" and then they go on to explain what land law is. [This] kind of irrelevant sloppiness . . . shows sloppy thinking.'

These methods – adding text in square brackets or using ellipses to indicate that text has been removed – must not be used to misrepresent the original, to try to convey a meaning that runs contrary to, or was not present in, the original text.

Sic

At times, you may quote something that itself contains a factual, grammatical or other error. Here, you should not correct the error; rather, the approach that is often taken is to insert the word *sic* (Latin for 'thus') in square brackets after the error. This indicates to your reader that you have copied the quotation directly, and that the error was in the original. For instance, a quotation might read: 'McGarry writes that, "Dogs is [*sic*] better than cats".' I should note, though, that some referencing guides ask you not to include *sic* or other commentary in the quotation itself, but to make such commentary in a footnote.

Long and short quotations

Short quotations should be part of your normal text. Longer quotations should be separated from the main text and indented. For instance, see Figure 10.6.

What amounts to a long quotation may be dictated by your law school's referencing guide. If not, the rule that is often adopted is that a quotation that is three lines or more in length should be separated from the main text and indented.

Text text text text text text. Text text text, 'quotation quotation quotation quotation'. Text text text text text text text text text text. Text text text text text:

> 'Quotation quotation quotation. Quotation quotation quotation quotation quotation quotation quotation. Quotation quotation quotation quotation quotation quotation quotation. Quotation quotation quotation quotation quotation quotation quotation.

Text text text text text text text text text text. Text text text text text text text text text. Text text text text text text text text text. Text text text text text text text text text.

Figure 10.6 Short and long quotations

Chapter 11
After your degree

This chapter will:

- discuss some of the main legal careers and the route that those with a qualifying law degree can take into such careers;
- consider careers outside legal practice that law graduates might pursue;
- provide advice on drafting CVs and covering letters to accompany job applications;
- discuss various postgraduate options that are available and explain how the various postgraduate degrees differ from each other.

11.1 INTRODUCTION

Most students will begin their law degree with the intention of becoming a practising lawyer, usually with the aim of becoming either a barrister or a solicitor.

However, whatever your initial career plans, they are not fixed in stone. You should feel free to change your mind if – during your degree – you think you would be better suited for, or would better enjoy, an alternative career than the one you planned when you first began your degree.

Throughout your degree, you should take the opportunity to discuss your career plans with those people in your institution whose job it is to advise you. These might typically include: your personal tutor, your law careers adviser and your institution's careers service.

This chapter aims to indicate some of the options that will be available to you after your degree. It cannot be a complete guide – that would take a book in itself.

Rather, it attempts to give you a taste of the choices you could make and how you can begin to find out more in order to pursue them.

The following advice assumes that you are taking, or will have completed, a qualifying law degree. With regard to practising law, it is applicable for those who want to practise in England and Wales; different rules and procedures apply in other jurisdictions.

11.2   GOING INTO PRACTICE

There are a number of routes to becoming a practising lawyer, and the following attempts to give you some idea of the commonest.

If you want to become a practising lawyer, you need to be realistic. Being a barrister might sound romantic (though it may not be in reality), but it is unlikely to happen if you are not a confident public speaker and you are not getting grades of 2:1 or above (though you can work to improve both your grades and your ability to speak in public). Similarly, you are unlikely to become a solicitor in a leading law firm if your attendance at class as an undergraduate – as stated in any reference provided by your lecturers – indicates a lack of commitment, and your grades indicate a lack of ability.

11.2.1 Barristers

Barristers are specialist advocates who will represent clients both in court and outside it. They also offer expert advice and opinions. Barristers are commonly self-employed, working from barristers' chambers with other barristers. Some, though, are salaried.

Following a law degree (which is referred to as the academic part of a barrister's training), a student needs to complete the vocational and practical stages of their training to qualify as a barrister.

The vocational part of a barrister's training consists of the Bar Professional Training Course (BPTC). The course is 12 months long for full-time students, or 24 months part-time. A student will usually be expected to have at least a lower-second-class law degree (a 2:2) to enrol on the course, though some providers will only accept those with a 2:1 or above. Before enrolling on to the BPTC, applicants must also have completed the Bar Course Aptitude Test (BCAT) and be a member of one of the four Inns of Court: Inner Temple, Middle Temple, Gray's Inn or Lincoln's Inn.

Following the vocational stage, the practical stage involves the completion of a pupillage, usually in a barristers' chambers. The pupillage is 12 months long, during which the pupil barrister will be assigned a supervisor. In the first 6 months, a pupil will shadow the supervisor, attending court and conferences with them and undertaking legal research and drafting. During the second 6 months, a pupil will take on their own cases, under supervision.

Following completion of the pupillage, the individual will become a barrister and will want to acquire tenancy: become a permanent member of chambers, either where they trained or elsewhere.

The following websites of the Bar Council and the Bar Standards Board contain further details about: taking the BCAT; joining one of the Inns of Court; taking the BPTC, including a list of course providers; and the pupillage gateway via which candidates may apply for pupillages:

* www.barcouncil.org.uk
* www.barstandardsboard.org.uk

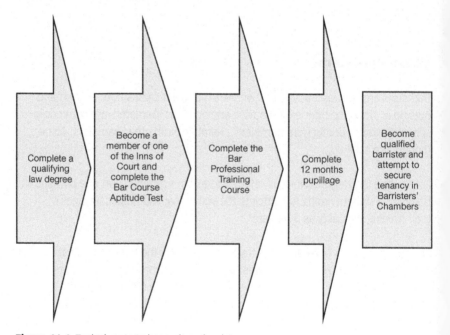

Figure 11.1 Typical route to becoming a barrister

Competition for pupillage and tenancy is very strong, and, in both cases, there are many more applicants than vacancies. In order to improve your chances, there are some elementary steps that you must take while an undergraduate.

You should take any opportunities you can to moot, both within your law school and externally, in competitions with other law schools. Some pupillage applications will ask about your mooting experience, and all will expect you to mention it. You can learn more about mooting in Section 8.2 of Chapter 8.

You should also attempt to secure some mini-pupillages. These are brief opportunities – a week or so – to shadow a barrister and to perhaps carry out some simple administrative work. Undertaking mini-pupillages will provide you with valuable insight and experience of life at the bar. It will also demonstrate your commitment to becoming a barrister and allow you to develop some valuable contacts. You can obtain mini-pupillages by enquiring directly of individual barristers' chambers, or even of individual barristers whom you may meet (if it seems appropriate). Some chambers even have a quasi-formal route of applying for mini-pupillages via their websites, so it is worthwhile doing an Internet search to try to find some.

If it arises, you should also take the opportunity to undertake work experience in a solicitors' practice. This will help you gain an insight into the work of solicitors and, again, help you to cultivate contacts among both solicitors and barristers (remember, solicitors will frequently come into contact with, and engage, barristers).

Finally, you should consider volunteering for organisations that offer free – or reduced-fee – advice, and sometimes advocacy, to members of the public. Organisations such as the Citizens Advice Bureau (CAB) or the Free Representation Unit (FRU) are ideal for this kind of voluntary work. The web addresses of these two organisations are:

- www.citizensadvice.org.uk
- www.thefru.org.uk

Your law school might also run a law clinic that offers pro bono (free) legal advice to members of the public. If so, you should try to become involved.

11.2.2 Solicitors

The role of solicitors is varied, but, generally speaking, they are often engaged in advising and representing clients. They may represent clients in court, and solicitors can obtain higher rights of audience to appear in courts at all levels. They may also represent in negotiations or simply by acting on behalf of clients.

At the start of their career, most solicitors are salaried, that is, they are paid a wage for working (usually, though not always) in a solicitors' practice. Later in their careers, many solicitors become partners in a law firm.

Following their law degree, those wishing to become a solicitor would take the Legal Practice Course (LPC). The entry requirements for the course vary from provider to provider, but most will expect you to have, or (if you have not yet completed your degree) be likely to obtain, a lower-second-class degree (a 2:2).

On completion of the LPC, students will next undertake the practice-based part of their training. This is on-the-job training (a little like an apprenticeship), usually in a

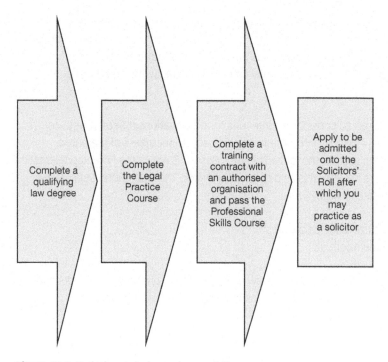

Figure 11.2 Typical route to becoming a solicitor

private solicitors' practice, though such training is available elsewhere – for instance, in government. To do this, you apply for a training contract with an organisation that is authorised to accept trainees (usually, a solicitors' practice). During this practice-based training, you will be expected to complete the Professional Skills Course (PSC), which builds on the skills learned during the LPC.

Following the successful completion of the LPC, your training contract and the PSC, you can apply to be admitted on to the roll of solicitors of England and Wales, which will allow you to practise as a solicitor.

You should access the Law Society's website for more information about: the LPC, including details of providers of the course; the practice-based part of the training (the training contract); and the PSC: www.lawsociety.org.uk

To enhance your chances of securing a training contract, you should:

- engage in any legal work experience that you can, such as in a solicitors' practice or by obtaining a mini-pupillage (which will give you valuable experience of an alternative branch of the profession and allow you to develop useful contacts);
- volunteer with organisations, such as the CAB, that offer free advice to members of the public; and
- if your law school has a law clinic that provides pro bono advice to the public, you should try to become involved in that also.

Figure 11.3 How to enhance career prospects

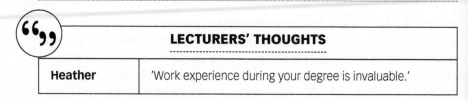

	LECTURERS' THOUGHTS
Heather	'Work experience during your degree is invaluable.'

11.2.3 Legal executives

The work of legal executives is very similar to that of solicitors. Like solicitors, legal executives will advise and represent clients. The primary difference between the two is that the practice-based training of legal executives is narrower: solicitors will receive practical training in a broad range of legal areas, whereas legal executives will usually specialise in the one area in which they wish to practise.

Legal executives usually train while in employment, and this route to becoming a practising lawyer is often more economical than training for a solicitor or a barrister, not least because the fees for completing the Graduate Fast-track

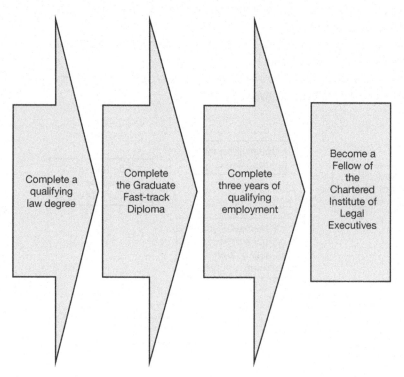

Figure 11.4 Typical route for law graduates to become a Fellow of the Chartered Institute of Legal Executives

Diploma (GFTD) to become a legal executive are a fraction of the cost of the BPTC or the LPC.

For those who have a qualifying law degree, the training requires them to complete the GFTD, which is typically completed in 9–12 months, part-time. In addition, in order to become a Fellow of the Chartered Institute of Legal Executives, you must complete 3 years of qualifying employment – that is, work of a legal nature that involves advising clients.

The website of the Chartered Institute of Legal Executives provides more information about the GFTD and appropriate qualifying employment: www.cilexcareers.org.uk

It is worth noting here that Chartered Legal Executives may, with some additional training, proceed to qualify as solicitors; the Law Society's website gives further details of this process: www.lawsociety.org.uk

11.2.4 The Government Legal Service

The information provided thus far has focused on those who may go on to train as a lawyer in private practice, say in barristers' chambers or in a firm of solicitors. It is possible, though, to undertake legal training in other organisations, such as work as an in-house lawyer for a particular organisation (several large (non-law) firms, for example, have their own legal department), or as a government lawyer in either central or local government.

The Government Legal Service (GLS) is a good example of such an employer. The GLS offers legal services, including advice and representation, to central government. More pertinently here, the GLS also offers opportunities for law graduates who want to train as either a barrister or a solicitor. The GLS also employs Fellows of the Chartered Institute of Legal Executives.

More information about the GLS and the training opportunities it offers may be found on its website: www.gov.uk/government/organisations/civil-service-government-legal-service

11.2.5 Paralegals

Paralegals carry out a broad range of legal work. For instance, paralegals are often employed in solicitors' practices to undertake various work advising clients. There are no formal qualifications necessary to work as a paralegal, though it is possible to obtain relevant paralegal qualifications.

Although some law graduates choose to work as a paralegal as a career end in itself, many do so as a means to gain some relevant, and paid, work experience and also to demonstrate their abilities and commitment to a potential provider of a training contract. In fact, working as a paralegal is often a good way to get your foot in the door of a legal practice, and it may lead to a training contract. In fact, some legal firms make it their policy to employ law graduates as paralegals, with a view to allowing them to apply for a training contract after, say, 12 months' employment.

	LECTURERS' THOUGHTS
Graham	'There is no longer a standard route into practice [as a solicitor or barrister]. It's sometimes useful to work as a paralegal – or to obtain other relevant experience – which will give you some idea of whether the profession is really for you. It will also allow you to get your foot in the door and earn some money before taking the LPC [or BPTC].'
Heather	'Students often leave university with the expectation that they'll do the LPC, go into a law firm and, immediately, run their own files and clients. They'd be better off getting some experience [of working in a law firm] before doing the LPC. There's more than one route to becoming a lawyer.'

11.2.6 Work experience

If you wish to practise as a lawyer, it is useful to acquire some relevant work experience while an undergraduate. Doing so will help you decide whether a career as a legal practitioner is really for you and may help you to decide what type of practitioner you would like to be. It will also allow you to develop useful contacts and to demonstrate your level of commitment to any future employer.

I have already noted in the above sections some appropriate work experience that you might want to carry out if you wish to work as a practising lawyer, and this section is simply the consolidation, and slight expansion, of that advice.

It is worth adding a note of caution about work experience here. Do not undertake work experience at the expense of your degree. You should not miss classes or fail to do the work for your degree because of work experience. Keep in mind that you are unlikely to become a practising lawyer – regardless of how much work experience you have – if your grades are poor or, worse, if you fail to complete your degree. I have witnessed one student who took on a number of mini-pupillages and, because of them, began to disengage from his law degree and, in fact, did not complete, or progress beyond, his second year.

COMMON ERROR

Do not miss classes or fail to do the appropriate work for your degree in order to take on work experience.

You should attempt to secure different types of work experience. Indeed, regardless of which branch of the profession you intend to enter, you should try to secure some experience in solicitors' practices and mini-pupillages.

You should also consider volunteer work with organisations offering free, or reduced-fee, legal advice or representation to the public. Organisations such as the CAB or the FRU are often looking for volunteers, and work of this nature will provide you with useful experience and will suggest a commitment to social justice that will be valued by many employers. The web addresses for the CAB and the FRU are given above, in Section 11.2.1.

Finally, as mentioned above, your institution may have its own law clinic offering pro bono legal advice to members of the public. Once again, becoming involved in such work will provide you with valuable experience and demonstrate to a potential employer your commitment to a career in law.

11.3   CAREERS OUTSIDE LEGAL PRACTICE

Many law graduates do not go on to practise law. There are many careers for which a degree in law is considered useful, including:

* in the police;
* in local or central government civil service;

- in journalism;
- teaching in schools or lecturing in further education; and
- in banking.

Indeed, a qualifying law degree is a high-value degree that equips you with a range of skills and knowledge that many employers see as desirable, including:

- oral communication skills;
- writing skills;
- legal knowledge;
- analytical and problem-solving skills;
- research skills; and
- the ability to evaluate competing arguments.

11.4   AN ACADEMIC CAREER

Some students may decide that, after their degree, they want to embark on an academic career, by which I mean that they will want to lecture or carry out research (usually both) at higher-education level.

Most academics are higher-education lecturers. The job of a lecturer comprises a number of roles. Commonly, lecturers:

- are teachers;
- are researchers (though it is possible to work in higher education on a teaching-only or research-only contract);
- provide pastoral care for students, whereby they provide emotional and educational support and advice; and
- engage in a variety of administrative tasks, from keeping accurate registers to managing degree programmes.

Strange as it may seem, there are no formal qualifications required to lecture in a higher-education institute. Most employers, though, will want you to have a further degree as well as your undergraduate degree – either a masters or a doctorate – or will want you to have experience as a practising lawyer. It is also most likely that you will also be required to undertake a Postgraduate Certificate in Higher Education (or similar qualification), though this is usually not a prerequisite, and you will normally be permitted to obtain this after you begin your employment.

Higher-education employers, such as universities, may also want to see evidence of your ability to research. To this end, there might be a requirement that you have a research degree or a portfolio of research (e.g. published articles or monographs).

If you are interested in becoming an academic, speak to one of your lecturers: they should be eminently qualified to advise you. You might feel a little foolish telling your lecturers that you, too, want to lecture; remember, though, that all your lecturers – regardless of how learned and formidable they might now seem – were once undergraduate students in the same position as you.

11.5   CVS AND COVERING LETTERS

Whichever career you decide to pursue, you will most likely be required to supply a curriculum vitae (CV) and a covering letter at some point.

Your CV should include:

- your name and contact details: your address, telephone number and email address;
- your educational qualifications;
- your employment history;
- any relevant experience;
- names and contact details of any referees (if required at this stage).

The details of your education and employment history should be arranged so that the most recent is listed first.

There are a number of principles you should bear in mind when drafting a CV and covering letter:

- Both the CV and covering letter should look as professional as possible and be completely error free in terms of grammar, spelling and general presentation. Often, employers will use CVs and covering letters as a quick, and brutal, way to filter job applications, consigning those that have any error whatsoever to the waste bin.
- Ideally, your CV should be no more than two sides in length, three at the most. Remember, the point of a CV is to allow a potential employer to scan it quickly to assess whether you are a suitable candidate for the job,

and they will not want to read pages and pages of information. For the same reason, you should avoid providing your information in dense paragraphs of text.

- You should print your CV and covering letter on good-quality paper. You should use a sensible font, a decent font size (usually font size 12) and black as the font colour. The presentation style should be professional and conservative (with a small 'c'), rather than showy and gimmicky.
- Your CV and covering letter should be tailored for each potential employer, focusing on their requirements. You will, of course, adapt CVs and covering letters that you have used in the past, but you must make sure that you change them sufficiently for each new application.

You should seek advice about drafting your CV and covering letter from your personal tutor, your law careers adviser and your institution's career service. You should also carry out an Internet search for appropriate examples of CVs, which may give you some ideas about how to structure and format yours.

11.6   POSTGRADUATE STUDY

There are a variety of reasons why you might want to engage in postgraduate study after your degree, including the following:

- You might want to gain a postgraduate qualification in order to make yourself more attractive to a potential employer.
- You might want to develop a specialism in a particular area of law.
- You might want to move on to a different career path for which a postgraduate qualification is necessary.
- You might want an academic career.

This section aims to give you a brief introduction to the different types of postgraduate study available.

Broadly speaking, there are four different postgraduate qualifications:

- postgraduate certificate
- postgraduate diploma
- masters degree
- doctorate.

The postgraduate certificate, postgraduate diploma and masters degree all involve study at the same level, though they differ in the amount required for each. Normally:

- a postgraduate certificate requires you to pass modules totalling 60 credits;
- a postgraduate diploma requires you to pass modules totalling 120 credits;
- a masters degree requires you to pass modules totalling 180 credits, and, often, 60 of those 180 credits must be obtained by completing a dissertation.

A doctorate is the highest category of degree awarded by higher-education institutions. The requirements of a PhD vary among institutions, but it is common that students must complete a substantial research dissertation of around 80,000 words (though, again, the specified length will be different in each institution and for different subjects). It is also common that the dissertation should amount to a significant and original contribution to knowledge.

11.6.1 Taught and research degrees

There are two basic types of postgraduate degree: taught and research. On a taught degree, most of the modules that are taken are taught – that is, you attend regular classes in particular modules (as you will have done for most of your undergraduate degree) and complete the assessments set by the lecturer. For a taught masters, as mentioned above, it is likely that you will also be required to complete a dissertation.

For research degrees, most of the degree will be earned by completing a substantial research project. There may be some taught elements of the degree: it is common, for instance, for students to have to complete at least one module in research methods and methodologies (see Section 9.7 of Chapter 9 for a brief introduction to research methods and methodologies).

Research masters degrees in law will usually be either an LLM by Research or an MPhil (Master of Philosophy). The distinction between these two degrees will differ from institution to institution. At doctorate level, students will usually undertake a PhD (Doctor of Philosophy). (Reference to philosophy in the MPhil and PhD degrees does not refer (necessarily) to the subject but, rather, refers to the general acquisition of knowledge and understanding.)

When you are deciding whether to do a research degree or a taught degree, the following points might be helpful:

- A research degree might offer more flexibility than a taught degree, simply because, with a research degree, you do not have to attend taught classes to the same extent as you do with a taught degree. Rather, much of a research degree is delivered via your engagement with your supervisors, which means that you can arrange mutually convenient times to meet them and even receive supervision by telephone, email or other forms of communication.
- On the other hand, some students would not want to study for a research degree, because they would miss the concrete framework that a taught degree offers and may not thrive as well with the flexibility of a research degree.
- A research degree might demonstrate your research potential better than a taught degree, which might be particularly valuable for those seeking an academic career.

There are two main paths on to a research degree. The first is that you produce your own research proposal, giving details of the research project you wish to undertake (Section 9.6 of Chapter 9 will give you some indication of what a proposal should contain). Often, with this first type, you can apply to any institution that has the capacity to supervise your project, though it may be that you apply to an institution that has particular expertise in the area of your proposed research.

The second is that you apply to complete a named research project designed by someone else, usually the person who will be on your supervisory team. This second type is usually advertised; candidates are asked to apply to the institution in question and to demonstrate some capacity to undertake the named research.

11.6.2 Discounts, bursaries, scholarships and other funding

Higher-education institutions will often offer financial help to students wishing to undertake postgraduate study. One of the commonest forms of financial help is for institutions to offer fee discounts to their own graduates; that is, you may be offered a certain percentage discount on the tuition fees if you undertake your postgraduate study at the institution from which you graduated.

Institutions also offer bursaries and scholarships to help pay tuition fees and, sometimes, living expenses. These are commonly awarded on a competitive basis, and you have to apply for them. Such awards may be restricted to certain types of student (e.g. those with a disability, with particular financial circumstances or from a particular background) or they may be open to everyone.

Another form of financial help that is becoming more popular is the role of graduate teaching assistant. With these, students combine their postgraduate study with some lecturing in order to gain teaching experience. Graduate teaching assistants are paid and will usually have their tuition fees paid for via the scheme.

Index

honours degrees and ordinary degrees 9–10

independent study 30–33; *see also* independent reading 32
internet 111, 133, 167, 178, 219, 228

journal articles 35, 49–51, 208–210, 211–212, 227

Latin terms: common 51–54; referencing 205, 206, 214
law reports: abbreviations 37–38; common features 39, 208–210; precedent 37; reading 36–37, 40–42; *see also* case reports 208
Law Society 221, 223
lecturers *see* academic staff
lectures 18–20, 22–26
legal executive 222–223
legislation 33, 42–44
LexisNexis *see* Westlaw and LexisNexis
literature review 180, 193, 196–197
LLB 2, 9

malpractice 60–65, 188
masters degrees 5, 172, 226, 228–229
markers: expectations in exams 126–128; first and second markers 9, 63, 88, 91, 94; what markers are looking for – coursework 88–95; what markers are looking for – presentations 145–146
marking criteria *see* assessment
methods and methodology 180, 181–183, 187–188
mini-pupillages *see* work experience
module leader 8; *see also* module convenor 8
monographs 32, 33, 36, 110, 111, 120, 227
moots: addressing the court and etiquette 166–167; mooting personnel 164; order of business 164–165; questions 167–168; rules 165–166

notes: after the lecture 25–26; note-taking 24

optional subjects: choosing 4–6
Oxford University Standard for the Citation of Legal Authorities 204, 210

paragraphs 116–117
paralegals 223–224
Parliament Acts 1911 and 1949 43
PhD 11, 172, 226, 228, 229
plagiarism *see* malpractice
planning your answer 97–106, 138, 147, 192
post-graduate study *see* further study
PowerPoint *see* presentations: presentation software
presentations: case names 156–157; dealing with nerves 159–160; delivery 159–161; handouts 156; legal authority 156–157; length of 146–147; practicing 158–159; questions 150–151, 155, 161–162; software 151–156; structure 147–148; talking speed 146–147
primary and secondary legislation 33, 213
primary materials 32–36, 99, 106–107, 110, 208; *see also* primary sources 32
principal lecturers *see* academic staff
problem questions: identifying issues 77–82; initial assumption 74–76; rubric 73, 76; unpacking 77–82
professors *see* academic staff
proofreading work 87–88, 121–123, 140, 190, 192
programme leader 8; *see also* programme co-ordinators or convenors 8
pupillage 164, 218–219, 221

qualifying law degree 2–3, 7, 217, 218, 220, 222, 223, 226
quotations, use of 64, 151–152, 156, 158, 213–215

readers *see* academic staff; *see also* associate professors 8
reading: and independent thought 106–111; before classes 19, 21, 23, 26–28, 30–32, 45, 168–170; benefits 32; for seminars 19, 26–28, 168–170; highlighting 49; variety 31, 33, 49–51, 91, 108–111
recording lectures 25
referencing: case law 205–208, 211; importance of 92–94, 201–203; repeat references 204–205; *see also* cross-referencing 205